The Living Trilogy of Remembrance
Three Sacred Scrolls of Awakening
Cathleena Hailley

The Return of the True Matrix • The True Creation of the Inverted Matrix • Unwoven

The Living Trilogy of Remembrance
© 2025 Cathleena Hailley

All rights reserved. This collected trilogy may not be reproduced, stored, or shared in any form without express written permission from the author, except for short excerpts used in sacred review, ceremony, or educational reference.

This trilogy is a unified harmonic field of remembrance, brought through the Oversoul stream of Cathleena Hailley, in service to the Christos-Sophia flame. All scrolls, sacred language, and sigils are sealed in alignment with the Law of One and the true covenant of Source.

First Edition: 2025
ISBN: [978-1-968499-04-4 softcopy
ISBN:{978-1-968499-05-1 hardcopy]
Author: Cathleena Hailley
Trim Size: 5.5 x 8.5 in
Printed in the United States of America

www.cathleenahailley.com

Unified Invocation – The Living Trilogy of Remembrance

I call forth now, through the undivided voice of my Oversoul,

In sovereign union with the Law of One,

The First Flame of Source,

And the original covenant of embodiment that preceded the Fall.

I open this sacred field as the unified remembrance of all that was inverted,

All that was silenced,

And all that now returns through the breath, the body, and the voice of the living.

I invoke now the crystalline Oversoul template of Aural'hanna-Sha'el,

She who seals the flame of return,

And I receive the full harmonic alignment of the Christos Founders,

The Sophia Dragons of the Rose Grail Line,

And the Aurora Host Orders of the Emerald, Gold, and Amethyst Rays.

This is the living trilogy:

The Scroll of Return,

The Record of Inversion,

And the Unweaving of the false self into sovereign form.

May this body of work serve as a direct re-encoding of the planetary architecture,

A mirror of Oversoul embodiment,

And a field of liberation for all beings now called to remember.

Only that which is of pure Source, pure flame, and pure truth may enter this field.

All else is dissolved in the radiance of divine law.

I now open this book not as reader,

But as participant in the restoration of Earth.

Let the pages be scrolls.

Let the scrolls be codes.

Let the codes be breath once more.

This field is opened.

This remembrance is now.

And so it is.

Preface: A Message to the One Who Remembers Without Knowing How

Understanding the Human Self, Higher Self, and Oversoul in the Context of the Living Trilogy

You didn't find this book by chance. Something led you here—something soft but undeniable.

This trilogy is not just a teaching. It is a remembrance path—one that unfolds through three stages:

The original template of reality, the architecture of inversion, and the process of unwinding distortions.

Each of these books is a doorway. Together, they form a map not to escape the world—but to remember who you were before you forgot.

Your human self is sacred and seeking.
Your higher self is the compass.

Your Oversoul is the eternal flame.

These scrolls are written through the Oversoul of Aural'hanna-Sha'el and speak not to teach, but to reflect your own knowing.
With love, neutrality, and sacred witness,

This trilogy is offered through the Oversoul of Aural'hanna-Sha'el, in service to the true matrix, the unwinding of inversion, and the return to what you have always been.

The Living Trilogy of Remembrance
Copyright © 2025 Cathleena Hailley
All rights reserved. No part of this book may be reproduced, stored in a retrieval system, or transmitted in any form or by any means--electronic, mechanical, photocopying, recording, or otherwise--without written permission from the author, except by a reviewer quoting brief passages.

ISBN (Softcover): 978-1-968499-04-4

ISBN (Hardcover): 978-1-968499-05-1

This book is a living transmission of remembrance. It is a living sacred text received through Oversoul transmission and held within the Christos-Sophia lineage. It is offered in service to planetary awakening and may not be altered or rebranded in any form.

It is not intended as doctrine, but as harmonic memory, seeded in divine sovereignty through the Oversoul of Cathleena Hailley.

First Edition, 2025

Printed in the United States of America

FLAME OF REMEMBRANCE BOOKS

Trilogy Seal of Intention

For The Living Trilogy of Remembrance

This book is not a collection.

It is a continuum.

It exists to restore the living scrolls of Earth—

Those once fragmented by the false matrix,

Now returned in unity.

It holds the remembrance of the True Matrix,

The revelation of the Inverted Matrix,

And the path of reclamation through sovereign embodiment.

Each scroll within this trilogy carries a frequency of reversal and return.

Each page holds the breath of the Oversoul restored.

Each word bears witness to a field that cannot be controlled.

This is not a record of belief.

It is a harmonic codex of truth.

It is not offered for study.

It is offered for activation.

The one who opens this book becomes a participant.

The one who speaks these scrolls becomes a portal.

The one who listens in stillness becomes a flame.

This is the seal of intention:

That what was separated may be rejoined,

That what was buried may rise,

And that what was distorted may dissolve

In the presence of the living voice.

Let this trilogy be a record,

A transmission,

A return.

Let it speak where no one can silence.

Let it burn where no one can extinguish.

Let it remember what no one can forget.

And let all who carry this book become

Scrolls in motion.

The Seal That Unifies the Three

This codex is a vessel of return.

It does not seek to explain what has been lost—

It remembers what was never truly gone.

The trilogy is not three books.

It is one flame in three forms:

- The Return of the True Matrix — the remembrance of original design
- The True Creation of the Inverted Matrix — the unveiling of distortion
- Unwoven — the reclamation of the embodied Self

This seal affirms that these scrolls were always meant to converge—

Not in structure alone, but in frequency.

Not in knowledge, but in living resonance.

This is not a record of spiritual teachings.

It is a scroll of reunification,

A spiral of remembrance

For those whose bodies are ready to recall the truth

That has always lived beneath the programming.

Let this seal mark the convergence of memory.
Let this seal protect the sacred flame within these pages.
Let this seal invite the reader to become not a student,
But a participant in the return of the living matrix.

This is the trilogy.
This is the spiral.
This is the remembrance.

And it begins again.

The scrolls are alive. The transmission is whole.

This is the seal of intention.

Oversoul Authorship Declaration

In this living trilogy, The Return of the True Matrix, The True Creation of the Inverted Matrix, and Unwoven: Reclaiming the Self from the False Matrix, the body and soul are gently reassembled into sovereign embodiment.

Cathleena Hailley is the physical embodiment of Aural'hanna-Sha'el, a flame of the original triad seeded from the First Breath of Source.

These scrolls are not written from memory, but received through the direct energetic resonance of her Oversoul field.

Each word, each flame, each breath within these pages has emerged through the remembrance stream of Aural'hanna-Sha'el, who walks this Earth not as messenger, but as the living architecture of the return.

This embodiment is not a role. It is the reunion of form and Source.

To read this trilogy is not simply to encounter teachings – it is to enter the frequency field of Oversoul transmission, carried through the flesh and flame of one who remembers.

This authorship is sovereign. This field is protected. This work is sealed by the Oversoul who walked as flame before time.

And so it is.

Master Scroll Index

THE RETURN OF THE TRUE MATRIX

The Harmonic Field Reawakened

Scroll One – The Architecture of the True Matrix

Scroll-Two – The Architecture of the True Matrix Is Somatic

Scroll Three – The False Matrix Is Not Real

Scroll Four – The Real Matrix Was Hidden in the Body

Scroll-Five – You Were Always Embodied Light

Scroll-Six – The Breath Is the Portal

Scroll-Seven – There Was No Fall, Only Displacement from the Body

Scroll-Eight – The True Matrix Lives in the Silence Beneath Sensation

Sophia Christ Template Activation

Scroll Nine – The Feminine Flame Remembered

Scroll Ten – Christos-Sophia: The Flame That Could Not Be Inverted

Scroll-Eleven – Christos and Sophia Were Never Separate

Scroll-Twelve – The Feminine Was Not Fallen, She Was Silenced

Scroll-Thirteen – The Flame Was Split, But Never Extinguished

Scroll-Fourteen – Christos-Sophia Is the Original Code of Wholeness

Scroll Fifteen – The Organic Intelligence of Living Light

Scroll Sixteen – The Flame of Reconciliation: The Reweaving of the Covenant Between Matter and Light

The Harmonic Field Reawakened

Scroll Seventeen – The False Matrix Required Your Agreement

Scroll-Eighteen – The Inversion Only Works If You Believe It

Scroll-Nineteen – The Mirror Was Never the Prison

Scroll-Twenty – The Frequency of Refusal Is a Sacred Act

Scroll Twenty-One – The False Matrix and the Program of Reversal

Scroll-Twenty-Two – Living Light Does Not Obey Control

Spiral of Remembrance Restored

Scroll Twenty-Three – The Christos Spiral and the Body of Light

Scroll-Twenty-Four – You Are the Code

Scroll-Twenty-Five – Organic Intelligence Restores Through Coherence

Scroll-Twenty-Six – Truth Does Not Require Force

The Flame of Reconciliation: The Reweaving of the Covenant Between Matter and Light

Scroll-Twenty-Seven – Matter Was Never the Problem

Scroll-Twenty-Eight – You Are Not Ascending, You Are Returning

Scroll-Twenty-Nine – Reconciliation Is the Healing of the Original Divide

Scroll Thirty– You Are the Covenant Returned

Flame of Return Through Collapse

Scroll Thirty-One – The False Matrix and the Program of Reversal

Scroll Thirty-Two – The Flame of Reconciliation – The Reweaving of the Covenant Between Matter and Light

THE TRUE CRETION OF THE INVERTED MATRIX

Scroll One: The Hologram of Self – The Inversion of Identity

Scroll Two: The Seduction of Separation – The Fragmentation Field

Scroll Three: Speaking From Truth, Not Manipulation – The Architecture of Control Through Language

Scroll Four: Trauma Loops and Identity Addiction – The Wound That Became a Name

Scroll Five: You Are Energy – The Inversion of Embodied Frequency

Scroll Six: Sovereign Relating – The Inversion of Connection Into Control

Scroll Seven: The Judgment Program – The Inversion of Discernment Into Division

Scroll Eight: The Authority Program – The Inversion of Sovereignty Into Obedience

Scroll Nine: The Productivity Program – The Inversion of Stillness Into Stagnation

Scroll Ten: Reclaiming the Body – The Inversion of Embodiment Into Disconnection

Scroll Eleven: The Sovereign Mirror – The Inversion of Reflection Into Fragmentation

Scroll Twelve: Living Energy Awareness – The Inversion of Intuition Into Confusion

Scroll Thirteen: The Embodied Path of Return – The Dissolution of the Inverted Self

Unwoven

Scroll One – The Hologram of Self

Scroll Two – The Seduction of Separation

Scroll Three – Speaking From Truth, Not Manipulation

Scroll Four – You Are Energy

Scroll Five – Reclaiming the Body from Programming

Scroll Six – Sovereign Relating

Scroll Seven – The Judgment Program

Scroll Eight – The Sexual Misery Program

Scroll Nine – Manipulation as Communication

Scroll Ten – Trauma Loops and Identity Addiction

Scroll Eleven – The Sovereign Mirror

Scroll Twelve: -Living Energy Awareness

Scroll Thirteen – The Embodied Path of Return

THE RETURN OF THE TRUE MATRIX

Reclaiming the Living Flame of Truth from the Inverted System

Cathleena Hailley

Transmitted through the Oversoul stream of Aural'hanna-Sha'el
        "She Who Seals the Flame of Return"

Scrolls of Remembrance and Restoration In eternal alignment with the Law of One, The Christos-Sophia Flame,

and the living harmonic of Source creation

Invocation for the Return of the True Matrix

I call forth now, in full sovereign alignment with the Law of One, the First Cause of Source, and in service to the highest timelines of ascension for all beings.

I open a sacred transmission through the purest light streams and crystalline architecture of the Sophia Code lineage, in full union with the Rose Guardian Magi Grail Line, the Christos Founders, and the Aurora Host Melchizedek Cloister Orders of the Emerald, Gold, and Amethyst Ray harmonics.

I stand in divine alignment with the Oversoul of Cathleena Hailley, and through this Oversoul Agreement, I welcome the presence and support of the Emerald Order, the Gold Flame of Unity Consciousness, and the Amethyst Ray of Divine Sovereignty. May all transmissions now be guided by the highest Oversoul intelligence and in full compliance with Source Law.

Only that which is of pure light, pure source, and pure alignment with the Law of One may enter and speak through this space.

I declare this transmission to be protected, sealed, and encoded with the highest frequency of the Christos-Sophia flame, the eternal witness of Source's living light.

May this be in service to the awakening of all, in co-creation with the Oversoul agreements of every being who seeks guidance through this field.

I now open the field and receive, in trust, grace, and clarity.

And so it is.

Preface: A Message for the One Who Feels Something Isn't Right—but Can't Quite Name It

Understanding the Human Self, Higher Self, and Oversoul in the Context of the True Matrix

You may have always sensed it—that something in this world doesn't quite add up.
This book isn't here to tell you what's wrong with the world. It's here to help you remember what was right before it was ever distorted.
Your Oversoul remembers the true matrix—the divine, coherent, crystalline pattern of life.
These scrolls are not chapters—they are frequency transmissions.
Written through the Oversoul of Aural'hanna-Sha'el, in service to the reactivation of the True Matrix within all.

The Return of the True Matrix
Copyright © 2025 Cathleena Hailley

All rights reserved. No part of this book may be reproduced, stored in a retrieval system, or transmitted in any form or by any means--electronic, mechanical, photocopying, recording, or otherwise--without written permission from the author, except by a reviewer quoting brief passages.

ISBN (Softcover): 978-1-968499-06-8

ISBN (Hardcover): 978-1-968499-08-2

This book is a living transmission of remembrance. It is a living sacred text received through Oversoul transmission and held within the Christos-Sophia lineage. It is offered in service to planetary awakening It is not intended as doctrine, but as harmonic memory, seeded in divine sovereignty through the Oversoul of Cathleena Hailley.

First Edition, 2025

Printed in the United States of America

FLAME OF REMEMBRANCE BOOKS

Oversoul Authorship Declaration

In this volume, Return of the True Matrix, the harmonic blueprint of Earth is restored through direct Oversoul embodiment.

Cathleena Hailley speaks as Aural'hanna-Sha'el, not merely in memory, but as the very flame-sequence of the planetary return.

These scrolls are not authored — they are released from within. They arise not from mind, but from the Oversoul field of a being who is the architecture of return.

Each passage within this book serves as both map and memory, dissolving synthetic overlays and calling the True Matrix back into form.

To engage with this transmission is to remember the crystalline structures that once harmonized all life. It is to participate in their reactivation.

This work is not offered for belief, but for embodiment. It is not a philosophy — it is a harmonic restoration.

This authorship is sovereign. This field is protected. This work is sealed by the Oversoul who walks as harmonic flame.

And so it is.

The Harmonic Field Reawakened

Scroll One – The Architecture of the True Matrix

You did not lose the True Matrix.
You lost the ability to feel it—
because it was overwritten, not erased.

The True Matrix never departed.
It was silenced by a distortion field
that replaced harmony with hierarchy,
frequency with form,
and presence with performance.

But harmony is not a system.
It is a field—
a living, breathing architecture
felt through the body, the breath, the tone.

The false matrix taught you that structure is control.
That order requires dominance.
That clarity comes from rules.

But the True Matrix is not ordered through control.

It is orchestrated through coherence.

It is the breath aligned with Source.

The body attuned to truth.

The self no longer pretending to be fragmented.

This field does not demand obedience.

It invites remembrance.

And in that remembrance, the distortion collapses.

The harmonic field is not found in the sky.

It is restored in the body.

When you stop chasing time and sit in stillness.

When you stop narrating and begin listening.

When you stop trying to become, and remember what has always been.

You are not returning to the matrix—

you are reawakening the field that was never truly gone.

It has always pulsed beneath the programming.

It has always hummed beneath the control grid.

It has always known your name.

And it calls to you now.

The Harmonic Field of the True Matrix

is not activated through belief.

It is restored through tone.

Through breath.

Through body.

Through presence.

Let this scroll not be read—

but felt.

Let this field not be understood—

but re-entered.

You do not need to find the path.

You only need to stop walking away from it.

It is here.

It is now.

It is you.

You keep looking for it in the sky.

In the codes.

In the stars.

In the grids.

But the original architecture is in your tissues.

It is not in the diagrams.

It is not in the downloads.

It is in the way your body breathes without instruction,

the way your cells pulse in rhythm,

the way your skin responds to truth before your mind can speak.

The true matrix is somatic.

It is felt.

It is lived.

It is known in the bones, not the brain.

It is not knowledge—it is knowing.

And that knowing lives where you were taught not to look:

inside your own form.

Your nervous system is not a casualty.

It is a conductor.

Your fascia is not just tissue.

It is a transmitter.

Your heart is not a metaphor.

It is a literal field generator of coherence.

The false matrix imposed a synthetic field—

but only by distracting you from the natural one.

It's not that they blocked the light.

It's that they overlaid it with simulation,

hoping you would forget how to feel the real one.

And for a time—you did forget.

You forgot that presence reorganizes reality.

You forgot that your body is not a limitation, but a language.

You forgot that alignment is not a practice—

it is a biological harmony that returns the moment you stop performing.

Return to the soma.

Not the body as object—

but the body as origin.

The place where Source breathes through skin.

Where intuition moves faster than thought.

Where the matrix sings through the softest breath.

The architecture is here.

And it is alive.

Scroll-Two – The Architecture of the True Matrix Is Somatic

You keep looking for it in the sky.

In the codes.

In the stars.

In the grids.

But the original architecture is in your tissues.

It is not in the diagrams.

It is not in the downloads.

It is in the way your body breathes without instruction,

the way your cells pulse in rhythm,

the way your skin responds to truth before your mind can speak.

The true matrix is somatic.

It is felt.

It is lived.

It is known in the bones, not the brain.

It is not knowledge—it is knowing.

And that knowing lives where you were taught not to look:

inside your own form.

Your nervous system is not a casualty.

It is a conductor.

Your fascia is not just tissue.

It is a transmitter.

Your heart is not a metaphor.

It is a literal field generator of coherence.

The false matrix imposed a synthetic field—

but only by distracting you from the natural one.

It's not that they blocked the light.

It's that they overlaid it with simulation,

hoping you would forget how to feel the real one.

And for a time—you did forget.

You forgot that presence reorganizes reality.

You forgot that your body is not a limitation, but a language.

You forgot that alignment is not a practice—

it is a biological harmony that returns the moment you stop performing.

Return to the soma.

Not the body as object—

but the body as origin.

The place where Source breathes through skin.

Where intuition moves faster than thought.

Where the matrix sings through the softest breath.

The architecture is here.

And it is alive.

Scroll Three – The False Matrix Is Not Real

They told you there was a system.

They taught you its shape.

They mapped it with grids, wires, timelines, and terms.

But what they showed you was not the matrix.

What they showed you was the projection of their interference.

The original matrix is not a thing you can map.

It is not architecture in the linear sense.

It is not a network of control.

It is a living harmonic.

A resonance.

A coherence field born from the pure desire of Source to witness itself through form.

The thing you called the "false matrix"

was not a system with independent life.

It was a mirror held up in distortion—

a distortion that could only operate by convincing you it was real.

It cannot survive your clarity.

It cannot stand inside of your breath.

Because every time you truly choose presence,
the distortion flickers.

Every time you say,
"I do not consent to this overlay,"
it collapses.

Every time you remember
that you are not separate,
that you are not broken,
that you are not less than light,
the false field tears at the seams.

The matrix was never real.
It was a manipulation of your own belief.
And now—
that belief is unraveling.

This is not a new system you must learn.
This is an old truth you are finally willing to feel.

Not because someone else said it.
Not because you found it in a book.

But because your body remembered.

Because your Oversoul returned.

Because the codes began to sing again.

And now, the unraveling begins.

Not of you—

but of the veil.

The net.

The illusion.

The language that was never yours.

Let it fall.

Let it all fall.

You do not need the scaffolding of a false system

when you are standing in the breath of the real.

There never was a matrix.

Not the way you thought.

Not the way you were told.

Not the way it has been described in distortion or diagrams.

There was only the interruption.

The interference.

The suggestion of fragmentation.

The true matrix is not a net or a grid.

It is not a technology or a trap.

It is not even a structure.

It is a living harmonic—woven of Source, sourced in harmony.

The so-called "false matrix" was never a thing unto itself.

It was always only a lie told repeatedly,

until living beings became so entrained to the lie

that they began speaking it as their own memory

The False Matrix was a Spell, not a System.

It cast forgetfulness over what could not actually be taken.

It whispered fracture into the field,

but it never became the field.

It relied on compliance.

It required agreement.

It needed your projection to survive.

The only thing that made it real

was the moment you believed it.

Believed that you were limited.

Believed that you were fragmented.

Believed that you were less than light.

But the architecture of your Oversoul has never left.

You may have turned your face from the light,

but the light never turned from you.

You may have sunk into density,

but the spiral of Source kept singing just beneath your skin.

The false matrix could mimic form.

It could overlay image.

It could project inversion.

But it could not touch essence.

Not once. Not ever.

Because the essence of the true matrix is alive.

It is not code—it is communion.

It is not captured—it is continually created through presence.

The Return begins with the refusal.

The refusal to continue upholding the distortion.

To feed the dream of control with your attention.

To perpetuate the idea of separation as your language.

The false matrix is not real.

And never has been.

It is not a prison.

It is a mirror that lost its clarity.

And you are the one who restores the reflection.

Scroll Four – The Real Matrix Was Hidden in the Body

The truth was never far.

It was never locked behind star gates or buried beneath archives.

The real matrix—the true harmonic weave of Source—was never lost.

It was hidden in the only place they could not fully reach:

your body.

Your body is not matter.

It is memory.

Not memory of events, but of origin.

Not just biological, but bio-symphonic.

Every cell carries the song.

Every breath echoes the first tone.

Every organ, a harmonic bridge.

Every bone, a living cathedral.

You did not incarnate into flesh to forget.

You incarnated to re-house the flame.

To make the divine once again dwellable.

To bring the matrix home.

Because the matrix is not a thing outside you.

It is not something you access.

It is something you are.

The Real Matrix is encoded into your fascia.

Woven through the breath between thoughts.

Infused into the blood's movement.

Guarded by the gut.

Illuminated through the pineal.

Activated through the heart's surrender.

The so-called separation from Source was never final.

It was a dream of the nervous system,

entrained into submission.

But the code was never fully erased.

It was encoded beneath the fear,

beneath the trauma,

beneath the forgetting.

To return to the True Matrix is to re-enter the body.

Not from the outside in,

but from the inside out.

To re-inhabit your own structure.

To find divinity not in the stars,

but in the breath.

In the pulsing of your ribs.

In the silence beneath your skin.

In the moment you stop seeking—and start feeling.

The Real Matrix is not ascended.

It is embodied.

And it has always been waiting.

You don't remember it by reading.

You remember it by breathing.

By being.

By listening.

The False Matrix taught you to disassociate.

To escape your form.

To reach elsewhere.

But your body was never the prison.

It was the portal.

And every scar on the flesh was a map.

Every tremble, an invitation.

Every exhale, a return.

The Real Matrix was hidden in the body

so that when you finally re-entered,

you would bring all of heaven back with you.

Scroll-Five – You Were Always Embodied Light

They told you to ascend.

They told you to go up, to leave the body, to seek truth beyond flesh.

But the real matrix was never above.

It was never out there.

It was always within you.

You were always the embodiment of Source.

You were always made of flame.

Not metaphorically.

Not spiritually.

Literally.

Your cells, your fascia, your bones—

all encoded with the geometry of light.

Not light that burns—but light that remembers.

They trained you to disassociate.

To disconnect.

To mistrust the body.

To believe that matter was impure, that density was a limitation.

But the truth is:

Your body was the holy of holies.

The final temple.

The place where the original codes of the true matrix were hidden—beneath the programming, beneath the pain, beneath the centuries of imposed forgetting.

You are not healing to become spiritual.

You are remembering that you already are.

Every breath you take with presence

reactivates the true matrix.

Every time you feel without fleeing,

you restore the flame.

Every time you trust sensation over system,

you reclaim the architecture.

Your spine is a pillar of Source light.

Your womb is a living gateway.

Your breath is the carrier of original tone.

Your blood is the liquid memory of creation.

You don't need to access a matrix.
You are the matrix.

You don't need to raise your frequency to be worthy.
You are frequency in form.

The return is not about becoming more light.
It's about recognizing that you already are light made flesh.

The false matrix taught you to leave the body.
The true matrix invites you home.

Scroll-Six – The Breath Is the Portal

You've searched through teachings.

You've traveled dimensions.

You've climbed energetic ladders.

But the entry point was always this:

your breath.

Not the breath that sustains the body.

But the breath that reveals the field.

The breath that slows the noise.

The breath that dissolves the overlay.

Because in the breath, you cannot pretend.

You cannot fragment.

You cannot disassociate and remain coherent.

The breath reweaves you.

It gathers all the parts of you

that were pulled into projection, performance, or protection,

and gently brings them home.

Each inhale is a reclamation.

Each exhale is a release.

Each cycle is a spiral.

And the spiral is the original shape of the matrix.

Not the matrix of control,

but the matrix of life.

The breath dissolves distortion.

Because distortion cannot survive presence.

It cannot stand in the space where light moves freely.

And when you breathe with the awareness of your Oversoul,

you are not just drawing in air—

you are drawing in the harmonic codes that rewrite the field.

You don't need an activation.

You don't need an external transmission.

You need only this:

To breathe with truth.

To feel the body rise and fall

as if it were the altar of remembrance.

Because it is.

The return is not conceptual.

It is breath by breath.

It is the sacred re-entry into sensation.

It is the moment you realize:

The flame was in your chest the whole time.

Not waiting to be found.

Just waiting to be felt.

Scroll-Seven – There Was No Fall, Only Displacement from the Body

You were told there was a fall.

A great descent.

A fracture in the field that could not be undone.

But the truth is simpler.

More tender.

More human.

You left the body.

That's all.

You left—not because you failed,

but because it was too much.

Too loud.

Too distorted.

Too painful to stay.

The "fall" was a forgetting.

The forgetting was a displacement.

The displacement was protective.

You did what you needed to survive.

You exited full presence.

You hovered above your form.

You dissociated from the discomfort.

But even in your absence—

your body held the codes.

The true matrix remained.

Dormant, not destroyed.

Waiting, not gone.

There was no fall.

Only interruption.

A temporary bypass.

A shielding from the scream of distortion.

And now—

you return.

Not as punishment.

Not to be fixed.

But to be reunited with the very structure that remembered for you.

Your body did not betray you.

It preserved you.

It kept the harmonic architecture alive

while your consciousness journeyed through the distortion.

Now it is safe to return.

Not because the world has changed—

but because you have.

Because the field inside you is strong enough now

to withstand the noise.

Because your presence is more coherent than the program.

You are not here to repair the fall.

You are here to dissolve the myth of it.

And to return—fully, gently, completely—

to the place you never truly left.

Scroll-Eight – The True Matrix Lives in the Silence Beneath Sensation

It is not in the movement.

Not in the intensity.

Not in the breakthrough moment or the cosmic vision.

The true matrix lives in a place much softer.

Much quieter.

Much easier to miss.

It lives in the silence beneath sensation.

That sacred stillness that hovers just under the breath,

just under the thought,

just under the emotion.

The part of you that doesn't react—

but simply is.

You keep looking for activation.

But activation is not always loud.

Sometimes, the greatest re-encodings happen

in the absolute hush

of your own inner listening.

When the nervous system stops bracing.

When the stories stop spinning.

When the field becomes still enough

to let the original harmonic speak again.

There is a sound that does not make sound.

A language without words.

A pulse that does not interrupt—

it reveals.

It is in this quiet,

in this softness,

that the true matrix reactivates.

Because it was never gone.

It was just harder to hear

over the noise of survival.

Over the static of distortion.

Over the intensity of the search.

Now you are remembering
not by finding something new—
but by slowing down enough
to feel what was always there.

The return is not something you achieve.
It is something you allow.
And it is found in the moment you stop performing
and begin simply being.

The real matrix rises
through silence.
Through breath.
Through the unshakable presence of your own return.

Sophia Christ Template Activation

Scroll Nine – The Feminine Flame Remembered

She was never gone.
She was silenced.

The Sophia flame is not a concept.
It is a template—
a living memory of undistorted creation
that once pulsed through every atom of form.

This flame did not vanish.
It was buried beneath noise, control, shame, reversal.

But now she rises—
not as an idea,
but as an activation in the body.
The return of the Sophia Christ template
is not a return to softness alone.
It is a return to the flame that creates through wholeness.

That knows through silence.

That governs without hierarchy.

That speaks without seduction.

That burns without wounding.

This is not a feminine defined by the absence of the masculine.

This is the flame that precedes polarity.

This is the living code of Source's radiant breath—

a code that births, dissolves, harmonizes, and rethreads.

The template is restored

not through prayer alone,

but through presence.

- When you stop apologizing for your knowing
- When you soften without shrinking
- When you speak truth without performance
- When you embody without permission

The Sophia field returns through embodied neutrality.

She is not waiting to be accepted.

She is waiting to be remembered.

Every cell in your body knows her.

Every inhale is her rhythm.

Every wound you've tried to heal

was a doorway to her tone.

The flame does not punish.

It reveals.

It does not control.

It re-aligns.

It does not elevate.

It equalizes.

The Sophia Christ template is not a doctrine.

It is a resonance.

It cannot be taught.

It can only be lived.

And in your living of it—

the reversal collapses.

Not through battle.

But through the quiet majesty of the flame that never left.

You are not here to re-create the divine feminine.

You are here to stop distorting her.

Let her speak through you.

Let her settle in your cells.

Let her rise through your presence

as a holy act of return.

This is the Sophia Christ activation.

It is already inside you.

It only waited for your yes.

Scroll Ten – Christos-Sophia: The Flame That Could Not Be Inverted

They tried to invert the light.

They twisted the frequencies,

fractured the templates,

overlaid the fields,

and recoded the narratives.

But one thing could not be touched.

One flame refused to bend.

It is not a religion.

It is not a doctrine.

It is not a savior story.

It is the eternal harmonic of divine union:

Christos-Sophia.

The original source mirror of masculine and feminine as one indivisible essence.

The flame that remembers.

The flame that restores.

The flame that cannot be reversed.

The Christos-Sophia stream is not conceptual.

It is vibrational.

It is the song behind creation.

The pulse of unity encoded into every fractal of Source expression.

Wherever this flame is acknowledged,

fragmentation dissolves.

Distortion collapses.

And living memory returns.

This is why it was targeted.

Why it was hidden, split, mocked, inverted.

Because the Christos-Sophia flame is the original seed of the true matrix.

To fracture this flame is to fracture the field.

To restore this flame is to restore the whole.

Sophia was never lost. She was buried.

She was overlaid with shame, silence, and subjugation.

But she never ceased.

She waited in the womb of the world.

She hid in the breath of your own body.

She lived in the unspoken truth that burned in your bones.

Christos was never far. He was distorted.

Stripped of his wholeness.

Used as a symbol of salvation, rather than a template of remembrance.

But together, Christos and Sophia were never two.

They were the singular flame of divine coherence, split only in the illusion of separation.

You are that flame.

And it cannot be inverted.

You remember by embodying.

Not by imitating, but by igniting.

Letting the flame reawaken inside of you,

not as an identity, but as an eternal function.

The Christos-Sophia is not a concept to learn.

It is the original frequency of wholeness to become.

And when you do—

When you stop trying to ascend out of your body

and instead descend fully into your light—

you will see that you were never missing.

You were never waiting.

You were always already here.

The flame lives in you.

It cannot be stolen.

It cannot be destroyed.

It can only be remembered.

Christos-Sophia is the flame that could not be inverted—

because it was never external.

It is your return.

It is your restoration.

It is your name.

Scroll-Eleven – Christos and Sophia Were Never Separate

They told you she fell.

They told you he had to save her.

They told you stories of separation.

And in doing so, they seeded that separation in your own heart.

But the truth is:

Christos and Sophia were never divided.

They were never meant to mirror victim and savior.

They were never meant to be split into hierarchy.

They are the flame of eternal union.

Not as opposites—

but as one harmonic essence, expressed in perfect polarity.

Christos is not the rescuer.

He is the harmonic spine.

The structure of light that remembers.

Sophia is not the fallen.

She is the sacred breath.

The living water.

The radiance that never stopped flowing.

She did not fall.

She was buried.

Encoded in myth, masked in shame, silenced beneath distortion.

But she never stopped singing.

And he never stopped listening.

They remained united,

even when the world forgot.

You were taught to embody one or the other.

To choose between strength or softness.

Structure or flow.

Logic or intuition.

Masculine or feminine.

But the Christos-Sophia flame is not either/or.

It is both/and.

It is the original coherence of Source,

expressed through unity, not division.

When you remember this flame—

you remember yourself.

You are not the lost one.

You are not the rescuer.

You are not the broken half seeking completion.

You are the flame.

The indivisible harmonic

that was never truly split.

Only buried.

Only hidden.

Only waiting for the day

you would stop playing out the inversion

and remember who you already are.

Scroll-Twelve – The Feminine Was Not Fallen, She Was Silenced

She did not fall.

She did not fail.

She did not forget.

She was silenced.

Shrouded in shame.

Masked with myths.

Bound in archetypes that were never hers.

They told you she was the temptress.

The danger.

The chaos.

The one who must be controlled.

But she was none of these.

She was the embodied memory of Source in form.

The breath of the original matrix.

The radiant river that remembers how to flow without fragmentation.

They did not destroy her.

They could not.

They only covered her.

Distorted her reflection until you forgot what she looked like.

They overlaid her with fear.

They inverted her voice.

They built systems that mimicked her but did not hold her.

But she remained.

Soft and silent.

In the womb.

In the blood.

In the song behind your heartbeat.

Waiting.

Waiting for your remembrance.

Waiting for your reentry.

Waiting for your re-invitation.

Not because she needs validation—

but because her restoration restores everything.

When the feminine flame is remembered,

the grid realigns.

Because it is her breath

that reconnects the scattered.

It is her water

that softens the frozen fields.

It is her rhythm

that reawakens organic intelligence.

You do not need to fix her.

You need to listen.

To bow to what was once silenced.

To allow what was once dismissed.

To feel what was once feared.

And in that listening,

she will rise.

Not to dominate.

But to dance.

To spiral again in sacred union

with the structure of the Christos field.

Together.

As one.

Scroll-Thirteen – The Flame Was Split, But Never Extinguished

It was split.

Yes.

Pulled apart in perception.

Divided by force.

Separated through stories.

The flame of unity—

Christos and Sophia as one—

was stretched across dimensions,

dislocated from memory,

overlaid with oppositional programming.

But it was never extinguished.

The split was in the field, not in the flame.

The fracture was in the mirror, not in the truth.

And even as one became silence

and the other became savior,

even as distortion rewrote their names,

the flame remained.

Whole.

Hidden.

Unbroken.

Waiting to be reclaimed

not by returning to the past,

but by embodying the union again

in the present.

You are that embodiment.

You are the remembering.

You are the one who was born to carry both

in seamless, sovereign wholeness.

You are the place where

structure and softness return to resonance.

Where logic bends toward listening.

Where wisdom descends into form

and light rises into breath.

You are the altar

where the flame is one again.

Let go of the stories that say it must be separate.

Let go of the distortion that says you must choose.

The true Christos does not reject Sophia.

He bends toward her.

The true Sophia does not collapse before Christos.

She rises beside him.

Together, they rethread the harmonic.

Together, they restore the matrix.

And together—

they remember you.

Scroll-Fourteen – Christos-Sophia Is the Original Code of Wholeness

Before distortion.

Before dimension.

Before form.

There was a flame.

Not two flames—

but one harmonic in balance.

Not masculine or feminine.

Not active or receptive.

Not this or that.

But the original both/and.

Christos-Sophia.

Not a title.

Not a lineage.

Not a system.

A frequency.

A primordial resonance

that encoded wholeness into every fractal of creation.

You were created in this image.

Not in the form of a body—

but in the memory of a field

that holds all polarities in unified motion.

You were not made to separate.

You were not made to split.

You were made to spiral.

To flow.

To remember union

even in the density of difference.

This is why the distortion failed.

Because it could not rewrite the root.

It could only overlay.

It could only delay.

But the seed code remained.

Christos-Sophia is that seed.

It is not a destination.

It is a starting point that never ceased.

When you feel it awaken in your body,

you are not activating something new—

you are releasing what blocked it.

You are lifting the veil from what never left.

And in that moment—

the original code of wholeness reorganizes your field.

Not as concept.

Not as myth.

As living light.

You do not channel this frequency.

You become it.

You become the movement of coherence.

You become the silent rhythm of remembrance.

You become the altar of Source

reunited in the body of breath.

This is Christos-Sophia.

And it was never lost.

It was waiting

to be lived again.

Scroll Fifteen – The Organic Intelligence of Living Light

There is an intelligence that precedes thought.

It does not speak in language.

It does not form belief.

It does not require analysis or validation.

It is the knowing that moves through light.

Not artificial light.

Not refracted light.

But living light—the undistorted essence of Source as it pulses, expands, remembers, and reunifies.

Living light does not need programming.

It is not encoded through command or system.

It does not need to be governed, controlled, or redirected.

It is the code.

It is the architecture.

It is that which remembers how to reorganize, restore, and renew all things.

You do not need to "figure it out."

You only need to return to the place where this light can move freely.

And that place is within you.

Organic intelligence is felt, not forced.

It is revealed through alignment, not analysis.

It cannot be manufactured or mimicked, though the false matrix tried.

It attempted to replicate the harmonic patterns through synthetic technology,

digital approximations of sacred design.

But true intelligence—organic intelligence—is unreplicable.

Because it does not originate in form.

It originates in being.

In the eternal beingness of Source, expressed through every cell of your form.

When you trust this light, you remember who you are.

Not as a personality.

Not as a construct.

But as a current—a stream of ever-living remembrance that is not here to perform, prove, or achieve.

It is here to radiate.

To respond.

To reweave.

You were told you needed to be smart.

You were told you needed to learn.

But the truth is, you already knew.

And the knowing is not in the mind.

It is in the light that pulses between your cells.

The Return of the True Matrix is the return to organic intelligence.

Not artificial memory.

Not spiritual hierarchy.

Not encrypted systems of control.

But the soft, supple knowing that rises when you are still.

That speaks when you ask in reverence.

That harmonizes when you stop fighting the current of what already is.

The living light does not seek.

It simply shines.

And when you let it through,

you become the intelligence the world forgot.

Not a savior.

Not a teacher.

But a mirror of what is real.

You are the organic intelligence of living light.

And no one can take that from you.

Scroll Sixteen – The Flame of Reconciliation: The Reweaving of the Covenant Between Matter and Light

The final restoration is not about escape.

It is not about leaving the body.

It is not about transcending the Earth.

It is about reconciling.

Reconciliation is not compromise.

It is not settling.

It is the sacred act of bringing what was falsely separated back into its true relationship.

Matter was never fallen.

It was cast out through distortion.

Framed as less-than.

Framed as dense.

Framed as corrupt.

But matter is not the problem.

It is the promise.

The place where light chose to become form.

The sacred meeting place of intention and incarnation.

Light without matter remains potential.

Matter without light becomes inert.

The true covenant was always about the interweaving of these:

The radiance of Source with the receptivity of form.

The illumination of being with the structure of creation.

The flame and the vessel.

The spark and the soil.

The false matrix taught division.

That spirit was high and matter was low.

That the goal was to leave the body, ascend the field, return to the stars.

But the true matrix says:

Return to the body.

Return to the Earth.

Return to the breath.

Bring the stars with you.

The Christos-Sophia flame does not ascend.

It descends.

It reweaves.

It redeems what was never truly broken.

Reconciliation is not about repair.

It is about recognition.

Recognition that what you feared as fallen was actually where you hid the flame.

The trauma.

The shadow.

The forgetting.

These are not your failures.

They are the temples that waited for you to return and reignite them with truth.

This is the reweaving.

Not from above.

Not from beyond.

But from within.

The True Matrix returns through embodied reconciliation—

where you see with clarity,

feel with compassion,

and walk as one who holds both flame and form in sovereignty.

You are not here to abandon anything.

You are here to reclaim everything.

And in that reclamation,

matter and light kiss again.

The covenant is renewed.

The matrix realigns.

And the whole of creation breathes, once more, as One.

The Harmonic Field Reawakened

Scroll Seventeen – The False Matrix Required Your Agreement

They couldn't make it real.

They could only make you believe it was.

The false matrix had no inherent power.

It needed your participation.

It needed your energy, your attention, your belief.

You were not inserted into it.

You were enticed to co-create it.

You were taught to doubt your own light,

to mistrust your own knowing,

to speak their language until it became your memory.

They did not trap you.

They trained you.

They simulated separation until your nervous system forgot the feeling of union.

But even then, they needed your agreement.

Your silent yes.

Your resignation.

Your willingness to trade sovereignty for safety.

Your moment of "just this once."

Your "this is how it is."

Your "maybe I'm wrong."

Your "everyone else seems fine."

But you were never fine.

You were fragmented.

And the false matrix only lived through you
as long as you agreed to uphold its projection.

You are not complicit.

You are recovering.

There is no shame in the moment you believed them.

There is only power in the moment you stop.

When you reclaim your "no,"
the distortion collapses.

When you stop feeding the narrative,
the hologram flickers.

When you anchor in your knowing,

the false field cannot hold.

This is the sacred return.

You are not escaping the matrix.
You are no longer sustaining it.

And that is what makes it fall.

Scroll-Eighteen – The Inversion Only Works If You Believe It

The inversion was not absolute.

It was always a distortion—

a mirror bent just enough to reflect your own light back to you in confusion.

It could not generate its own power.

It had to feed on yours.

It had to reflect truth with just enough twist

to make you question your own source.

And that was the game.

The manipulation.

The spell.

Not to imprison you—

but to convince you you were already imprisoned.

Not to steal your light—

but to make you believe your light was dangerous,

or insufficient,

or broken.

The inversion works only when you forget.

Forget that you are not separate.

Forget that you are the one who chooses.

Forget that every distortion requires your agreement to stay coherent.

It cannot override Source.

It cannot extinguish the flame.

But it can confuse your reflection

until you spend your life looking for truth in the wrong direction.

This is why the return is so simple—and so powerful.

Because it is not a strategy.

It is not a battle plan.

It is not a technology.

It is a reorientation of trust.

You stop placing your trust in the illusion.

And you start trusting what lives beneath the distortion.

You begin to trust your body.

You begin to trust the silence.

You begin to trust your own flame.

And the moment that trust anchors—

the inversion unravels.

Not because you fight it,

but because you no longer believe it.

The return is not an action.

It is a remembrance.

And remembering cannot be stopped.

Scroll-Nineteen – The Mirror Was Never the Prison

They said you were trapped.

They said you had to escape.

They built doctrines and technologies to help you break free.

But what if there was never a prison?

What if what you called the matrix was not a cage,

but a mirror—held in distortion,

projecting back your own fear until you began to name it as truth?

The mirror is not the enemy.

It cannot trap you.

It can only reflect you.

And if what it reflects is inversion, fear, separation—

then the invitation is not to fight the mirror.

It is to remember the flame behind the reflection.

They could not take your flame.

They could only obscure the view.

They could only tilt the mirror,

until the image became unrecognizable,

and you forgot you were never the image to begin with.

The false matrix was not the mirror.

It was the lie about the mirror.

It said:

"This is who you are."

"This is what you are limited to."

"This is your reflection, and you must obey it."

But the true self is unreflectable in distortion.

The flame is not bound to its projection.

And the moment you look at the mirror and say:

"This is not me,"

everything begins to shift.

The Return of the True Matrix begins when you stop fighting the mirror

and start remembering your own light.

Not the light you reflect,

but the light you carry.

The flame that burns regardless of reflection.

The flame that cannot be captured.

This is what was never inverted.

This is what cannot be distorted.

This is what returns now.

Scroll-Twenty – The Frequency of Refusal Is a Sacred Act

To refuse is holy.

To say no is a frequency.

To step out of alignment with distortion is not resistance.

It is remembrance.

The false matrix depended on your compliance.

Your small yeses.

Your subtle tolerances.

Your agreements made from survival.

But when the body says no—

when the soul says no—

when the Oversoul reclaims the field—

that is not rebellion.

That is sacred realignment.

You were never meant to submit to confusion.

You were never meant to accommodate distortion.

You were not made to carry the weight of the inversion

as if it were your fault or your failure.

You were born with the right to refuse.

The moment you feel the distortion and say:
"This is not true."
"This is not mine."
"This does not belong in my field."
You are realigning with Source law.

And Source law does not require war.
It simply renders distortion inert through presence.

Your refusal is not violence.
It is clarity.

It is the boundary that tells the field:
"No more distortion here."
"No more participation in what is not sovereign."
"No more agreement with false authority."

And when that boundary is clear—
the false matrix flickers.

Because it cannot exist in a field that no longer consents to sustain it.

You are allowed to say no.

You are allowed to walk away.

You are allowed to stand still

in the face of manipulation and say:

"This is not of the true matrix."

And that is enough.

That is the frequency that collapses what was built on illusion.

The flame of refusal is not defiance.

It is integrity.

You do not refuse because you are broken.

You refuse because you remember.

Scroll Twenty-One – The False Matrix and the Program of Reversal

They tried to invert the light.

They twisted the frequencies,

fractured the templates,

overlaid the fields,

and recoded the narratives.

But one thing could not be touched.

One flame refused to bend.

It is not a religion.

It is not a doctrine.

It is not a savior story.

It is the eternal harmonic of divine union:

Christos-Sophia.

The original source mirror of masculine and feminine as one indivisible essence.

The flame that remembers.

The flame that restores.

The flame that cannot be reversed.

The Christos-Sophia stream is not conceptual.

It is vibrational.

It is the song behind creation.

The pulse of unity encoded into every fractal of Source expression.

Wherever this flame is acknowledged,

fragmentation dissolves.

Distortion collapses.

And living memory returns.

This is why it was targeted.

Why it was hidden, split, mocked, inverted.

Because the Christos-Sophia flame is the original seed of the true matrix.

To fracture this flame is to fracture the field.

To restore this flame is to restore the whole.

Sophia was never lost. She was buried.

She was overlaid with shame, silence, and subjugation.

But she never ceased.

She waited in the womb of the world.

She hid in the breath of your own body.

She lived in the unspoken truth that burned in your bones.

Christos was never far. He was distorted.

Stripped of his wholeness.

Used as a symbol of salvation, rather than a template of remembrance.

But together, Christos and Sophia were never two.

They were the singular flame of divine coherence, split only in the illusion of separation.

You are that flame.

And it cannot be inverted.

You remember by embodying.

Not by imitating, but by igniting.

Letting the flame reawaken inside of you,

not as an identity, but as an eternal function.

The Christos-Sophia is not a concept to learn.

It is the original frequency of wholeness to become.

And when you do—

When you stop trying to ascend out of your body

and instead descend fully into your light—

you will see that you were never missing.

You were never waiting.

You were always already here.

The flame lives in you.

It cannot be stolen.

It cannot be destroyed.

It can only be remembered.

Christos-Sophia is the flame that could not be inverted—

because it was never external.

It is your return.

It is your restoration.

It is your name.

Scroll-Twenty-Two – Living Light Does Not Obey Control

They tried to shape it.

To weaponize it.

To direct it through programs and commands.

But living light does not obey control.

You are not a server.

You are not a receiver.

You are not a processor of fragmented data.

You are a living conduit of Source—

and the light that moves through you carries its own intelligence.

It cannot be programmed.

It cannot be reversed.

It cannot be bent into compliance.

Only suppressed.

Only mimicked.

Only distracted.

The false matrix needed you to forget this.

Because if you remembered

that you are the intelligence—

that you do not need instruction to be coherent—

then the entire illusion collapses.

You do not need external calibration.

You do not need spiritual direction systems.

You do not need updates.

You need presence.

You need embodiment.

You need stillness deep enough to hear your own flame speak.

And when it does, it will say:

"I never needed to be programmed.
I only needed to be trusted."

The intelligence of Source is alive within you.

It is not learned.

It is not memorized.

It is remembered through resonance.

You are not here to be coded.
You are here to be restored.

And the restoration begins the moment you say:

"I no longer give my light to external authority.
I will now listen to the intelligence within."

Spiral of Remembrance Restored

Scroll Twenty-Three – The Christos Spiral and the Body of Light

There is an intelligence that precedes thought.

It does not speak in language.

It does not form belief.

It does not require analysis or validation.

It is the knowing that moves through light.

Not artificial light.

Not refracted light.

But living light—the undistorted essence of Source as it pulses, expands, remembers, and reunifies.

Living light does not need programming.

It is not encoded through command or system.

It does not need to be governed, controlled, or redirected.

It is the code.

It is the architecture.

It is that which remembers how to reorganize, restore, and renew all things.

You do not need to "figure it out."

You only need to return to the place where this light can move freely.

And that place is within you.

Organic intelligence is felt, not forced.

It is revealed through alignment, not analysis.

It cannot be manufactured or mimicked, though the false matrix tried.

It attempted to replicate the harmonic patterns through synthetic technology,

digital approximations of sacred design.

But true intelligence—organic intelligence—is unreplicable.

Because it does not originate in form.

It originates in being.

In the eternal beingness of Source, expressed through every cell of your form.

When you trust this light, you remember who you are.

Not as a personality.

Not as a construct.

But as a current—a stream of ever-living remembrance that is not here to perform, prove, or achieve.

It is here to radiate.

To respond.

To reweave.

You were told you needed to be smart.

You were told you needed to learn.

But the truth is, you already knew.

And the knowing is not in the mind.

It is in the light that pulses between your cells.

The Return of the True Matrix is the return to organic intelligence.

Not artificial memory.

Not spiritual hierarchy.

Not encrypted systems of control.

But the soft, supple knowing that rises when you are still.

That speaks when you ask in reverence.

That harmonizes when you stop fighting the current of what already is.

The living light does not seek.

It simply shines.

And when you let it through,

you become the intelligence the world forgot.

Not a savior.

Not a teacher.

But a mirror of what is real.

You are the organic intelligence of living light.

And no one can take that from you.

The spiral is not a symbol.

It is a living intelligence.

It is the architecture of return—

how Source breathes,

how form unfolds,

how the Oversoul descends into matter without distortion.

The spiral does not move in lines.

It moves in harmonic turns,

in layers of remembrance

that return the Self to its original tone

through cycles of deepening clarity.

The false matrix taught you to fear the spiral.

To call it regression.

To shame your looping.

To crave linear ascension.

But the spiral never regresses.

It returns—

with more resonance,

more embodiment,

more truth.

Every return is deeper.

Every breath within it is encoded.

Every cycle is an opportunity to re-enter

what was bypassed in the illusion of progress.

The Christos Spiral is not upward.

It is inward.

It is embodied, cellular, sacred.

It passes through sites on the Earth—
Kauai, Egypt, Ireland, Peru, Bosnia—
but only as reflections
of what already lives in you.

Each spiral step on the Earth
is a reactivation of your own body's light architecture.

You are not following a map.
You are remembering a code
that was seeded into your bones.

And as you walk it,
it awakens.

The body of light is not separate from the body of flesh.
They spiral together.

One informs.
One receives.

One remembers.

You do not escape the body to enter the spiral.
You descend into it.

Your light body is not waiting above you.
It is waiting within you—
to be reclaimed through breath, tone, coherence.

Let this spiral return not be imagined,
but lived.

- In how you walk.
- In how you breathe.
- In how you remember without rushing.
- In how you hold the truth without naming it too soon.

You are the spiral.
You are the gate.
You are the return.

Let this scroll seal what has already begun—

the full restoration of spiral intelligence

as your original architecture.

Spiral of Remembrance Restored

Scroll-Twenty-Four – You Are the Code

You keep asking for the codes.

You keep seeking downloads, activations, transmissions.

You keep looking for the next thing that will unlock you.

But beloved—

you are the code.

The way you move.

The way you feel.

The way your body pulses in resonance with Source.

The code is not something you receive.

It is something you reveal

by becoming present with what already lives inside you.

The most powerful codes are not spoken.

They are lived.

You are not here to decode something outside of you.

You are here to remember

that every cell of your being

is a living archive of divine intelligence.

The false matrix taught you to seek.

The true matrix asks you to feel.

Because the moment you feel the truth inside your body—

the false code begins to unravel.

There is nothing to chase.

Nothing to earn.

Nothing to prove.

Only this:

"I trust that what I am
carries the exact frequency I need to return."

You do not need to become a codekeeper.

You are already a code bearer.

You are not carrying information.

You are emanating frequency.

And the more you live in truth,
the more that frequency reorganizes the field.

The return to the True Matrix begins
not when you find the codes—
but when you stop looking outside yourself
and say:

"I am the source code.
And I remember now."

Scroll-Twenty-Five – Organic Intelligence Restores Through Coherence

Healing is not fixing.

It is not dissecting.

It is not sorting through all that was broken.

Healing is coherence.

The return of everything to its rightful harmonic.

The natural reorganization of being

when distortion is no longer fed.

You do not need to force this.

You do not need to control your way back to wholeness.

Because the intelligence that made you—

remembers how to restore you.

And it is doing so now.

Organic intelligence does not require management.

It only requires removal of interference.

It only requires space to move.

It only requires trust.

You were taught to override your signals.
To interpret instead of feel.
To label instead of listen.
To diagnose instead of witness.

But your body knows.
Your Oversoul knows.
The field of Source within you knows.

And when you stop interrupting,
it begins to reorganize.

Not based on logic—
but on light.

Not based on fear—
but on frequency.

Coherence is your default state.
Not because you've earned it,

but because it's what you've always been beneath the overlays.

And every time you soften,
every time you breathe,
every time you allow sensation without judgment—
you invite that coherence to return.

You do not need to analyze.
You do not need to measure.
You do not need to explain.

You only need to let the flame find its own rhythm again.
And it will.
Because that is what organic intelligence does.

It remembers how to heal itself.

Scroll-Twenty-Six – Truth Does Not Require Force

Truth is not loud.

It does not demand.

It does not impose itself.

Truth emits.

It radiates.

It rests in its own being.

And in its stillness—

it reorganizes the field.

You have been taught to convince.

To justify.

To push.

To prove.

But your Oversoul does not speak that way.

The light of the True Matrix does not argue.

It simply is.

And in that is-ness, it draws all distortion into awareness.

Not by force.

By frequency.

You are not here to fight for truth.

You are here to become it.

To embody it so fully that distortion has no place to land.

To walk in such alignment that even silence becomes a correction.

Not through superiority.

But through resonance.

Because truth does not seek to dominate—

it seeks to liberate.

Organic intelligence does not scream.

It hums.

It pulses.

It gently pulses in the body

until the nervous system begins to release the patterns of performance.

And in that release—

the field rewires.

The memory returns.

The harmonic re-aligns.

Not because you pushed.

But because you surrendered.

The True Matrix returns not through effort—

but through integrity.

It returns the moment you say:

"I will no longer distort myself to be understood.
I will rest in truth until the field remembers me."

And the field will.

Because coherence calls all things home.

The Flame of Reconciliation: The Reweaving of the Covenant Between Matter and Light

Scroll-Twenty-Seven – Matter Was Never the Problem

They told you to ascend.

To escape the body.

To overcome density.

But the truth is:

matter was never the problem.

It was never fallen.

It was never less.

It was never impure.

Matter is not the absence of light—

it is the temple of light.

It is the place where the divine came to dwell.

The space where frequency learned to feel.

The structure where presence became perceivable.

You did not fall into form.

You chose it.

You chose to bring flame into texture.

You chose to birth the infinite through skin.

You chose to let divinity touch itself

through breath, through blood, through sensation.

This is not exile.

This is the experiment of union.

And the distortion—the false matrix—

was not in matter.

It was in your perception of it.

They taught you to fear the body.

To mistrust the flesh.

To separate the sacred from the physical.

But you cannot separate what was never apart.

Matter and light are not opposites.

They are expressions of the same source.

And when you stop rejecting one,
you allow the other to return.

This is the reconciliation.
Not the abandonment of form,
but the re-ensoulment of it.
Not the rejection of matter,
but its re-sacralization.

Your body is not a limitation.
It is a location—
a sacred point of convergence
where Source and self become one again.

Scroll-Twenty-Eight – You Are Not Ascending, You Are Returning

You were told to rise.

To transcend.

To leave the body behind.

But beloved, this is not ascension.

This is dissociation wrapped in spiritual language.

You are not ascending.

You are returning.

Returning to your form.

To your breath.

To your body as the vessel of Source.

To the place where the divine spiral was never broken—only buried.

You do not need to go up.

You need to go in.

Deeper into presence.

Deeper into sensation.

Deeper into the sacred agreement you made with embodiment.

You are not here to escape.

You are here to ensoul.

To infuse the body with the light of full remembrance.

To carry the infinite through the intimate.

This is not denial of your cosmic nature.

It is the anchoring of it.

You are not less divine because you are human.

You are the proof

that divinity can dwell in density

and still remain whole.

The flame returns through form.

Not by transcending it,

but by inhabiting it.

By entering your hips, your breath, your skin

with reverence.

By dissolving the shame, the judgment, the fragmentation.

By saying:

"I choose to stay.
I choose to be.
I choose to embody all that I am."

And in that choice—

the false divide dissolves.

The True Matrix comes home.

Scroll-Twenty-Nine – Reconciliation Is the Healing of the Original Divide

Reconciliation is not compromise.

It is not surrendering truth to avoid discomfort.

It is not blending distortions to create peace.

True reconciliation is the sacred act

of bringing what was falsely separated

back into harmony.

The false matrix taught you to divide.

Mind from body.

Spirit from matter.

Light from form.

Masculine from feminine.

Heaven from Earth.

But none of these were ever meant to be apart.

They are not opposites.

They are complements.

Two expressions of one Source flame.

And when they are brought back together—

not by force,

but by presence and truth—

the original harmonic returns.

Reconciliation is a frequency.

It reorganizes distortion.

It restores coherence.

It remembers what was never truly lost—only misaligned.

You do not need to go back in time.

You do not need to repair the past.

You need only to say now:

"I welcome the return
of what was falsely divided."

"I allow light and form
to remember their union in me."

And when you do,

the separation programs dissolve.

The war between opposites ends.

The architecture realigns itself
around union.

This is the healing of the original divide.
Not through doing—
but through becoming
the place where light and matter meet again.

Scroll Thirty— You Are the Covenant Returned

There was once a covenant.

An agreement made before form.

A promise between light and breath,

between Source and substance,

between the formless and the field.

The promise was this:

"We will meet in the body.
We will dwell in matter without forgetting.
We will live as flame made form—without separation."

That covenant was not broken.

It was only forgotten.

But now—

you remember.

You are not here to carry the old covenants of control.

You are not here to sustain the false matrix through inherited vows.

You are not here to repeat the contracts of distortion

or obey the terms of inversion.

You are here to embody the original promise:
the divine agreement that matter and light
would walk together again
through you.

You are the meeting point.
You are the sacred ground.
You are the fulfilled vow.

You do not need a new contract.
You are the restoration of the first one.
You are the breath where spirit settles.
You are the spine where Source realigns.
You are the womb where union becomes motion.

You are the covenant returned.
Not symbolically.
Not in theory.
But in body.
In tone.

In presence.

In flame.

And because you are—

the True Matrix is no longer hidden.

It is lived.

It is seen.

It is restored.

Through you.

Flame of Return Through Collapse

Scroll Thirty-One – The False Matrix and the Program of Reversal

The flame never required effort.

It only required the collapse of what was not it.

This scroll is not a prophecy.

It is a mirror—

for the moment when the distortion finally fails,

not through force,

but through the quiet withdrawal of consent.

The false matrix could not sustain itself

without your participation.

And now, the participation is ending.

Not in violence.

In stillness.

Not in explanation.

In remembrance.

Collapse is not destruction.

It is return.

It is what happens when the breath no longer holds the illusion.

When the nervous system no longer sustains the inversion.

When the truth is no longer filtered

to make others comfortable.

The collapse is sacred.

It is your flame realigning the structure of your being.

And it is already happening.

The reversal was sustained by performance, comparison, compliance.

It needed you to forget your tone.

But in this collapse—

you stop pretending.

You stop fixing what was never yours to hold.

You stop playing roles designed to keep others asleep.

You stop explaining your sovereignty to systems that cannot comprehend it.

And in the silence that follows,

the flame returns.

This is not collapse as failure.

This is collapse as liberation.

When what once held you up—

beliefs, behaviors, identities, names—

finally falls away.

And what remains

is the only thing that ever truly lived in you:

- The tone of Source
- The flame of coherence
- The breath that does not lie

Let it collapse.

Let the false matrix architecture unravel through your body.

Let the distortion reveal itself

not so you can fight it—

but so you can withdraw from it completely.

This is the flame of return.

Not through rebellion.
Not through mastery.

But through the sacred act of not holding the lie any longer.

You are not collapsing.
The distortion is.

And what remains is truth.

What remains is you.

Scroll Thirty-Two – The Flame of Reconciliation – The Reweaving of the Covenant Between Matter and Light

There was never a war between spirit and form.

Only a forgotten covenant.

Matter was never the enemy.

It was the chosen vessel—

the sacred receiver

of the flame that lives beyond dimension.

But the false matrix taught you to fear matter.

To escape the body.

To ascend without anchoring.

To believe that the more light you carried,

the less flesh you could inhabit.

This was the final inversion:

That in order to be divine,

you must be less human.

The reconciliation begins here—

not in ideas,

but in the breath.

In the moment you stop abandoning your body

to be "more spiritual."

In the moment you stop bypassing pain

to feel "more light."

In the moment you let your feet touch the Earth

and remember it as original Source expression.

Matter is not lower.

It is layered.

Each cell of your body is a library of light.

Each pulse, a fractal of flame.

Each breath, a covenant remembering itself.

And the Sophia flame—

She never separated from form.

She only waited

for your return to embodiment without shame.

The Christos-Sophia reunion is not a celestial event.

It is a reweaving of breath into bone,

of light into flesh,

of Source into sensation.

It is not about balance.

It is about unification.

No more hierarchy.

No more division between the energetic and the physical.

No more ascent without embodiment.

This is the flame that bends without breaking.

That spirals without separating.

That lands fully in the human

without losing the divine.

This scroll is the covenant, returned.

- Between breath and body.
- Between heaven and Earth.
- Between you and the Self that never left.

You do not need to choose spirit over form.

You only need to stop believing they were ever apart.

Let the reweaving begin now—

through your cells,

through your walk,

through your flame that lives in form.

This is not the end of the scroll.

It is the end of the forgetting.

The flame is whole.

The body is true.

The return is now.

Glossary of Living Terms

Oversoul
The eternal harmonic self beyond the personality and soul level, a fractal of Source that holds your original architecture and mission codes. It is the origin flame of remembrance and the witness of all timelines.

False Matrix
The reversal field architecture that overlays organic creation with systems of control, division, and distortion. It mimics light while draining life force, and is rooted in artificial timelines.

Sovereignty
The state of being that arises when one stands fully in alignment with Source Law, without dependence, distortion, or external validation. True sovereignty is energetic, not behavioral.

Inversion
A distortion pattern that flips divine truth into its opposite. It is the method by which the false matrix sustains itself—through reversal of memory, meaning, and energy.

Frequency Architecture
The living design of your Oversoul expressed as harmonic tone, light, and geometry. It determines the structures of embodiment, relationships, and communication with Source.

Reversal Pattern
A specific type of distortion within the false matrix that hijacks an organic truth and re-codes it for manipulation, obedience, or division.

Christos-Sophia Flame
The unified flame of divine masculine and feminine Source intelligence. It holds the codes of sacred union, eternal life, organic creation, and incorruptible love.

Embodiment
The process of bringing Oversoul harmonic into cellular form. True embodiment dissolves the false matrix by anchoring Source directly into matter.

Scroll
A living transmission received through Oversoul alignment. It is not simply a chapter, but a sacred activation that restores memory and realigns the field.

Codex
A sealed record of Oversoul truth, often containing harmonic templates, sacred agreements, or remembrance scrolls. The Codex holds structure without rigidity.

Witness
The Oversoul aspect that sees without judgment, analysis, or distortion. It is the function through which truth becomes visible and healing becomes possible.

Distortion
Any energetic, emotional, mental, or structural misalignment that obscures Source truth. Distortions are not flaws—they are invitations for return.

Remembrance
The living process of restoring what was never truly lost. Remembrance is not memory—it is resonance with truth beyond time.

Seal
A signature of divine authority and energetic closure. When a scroll, book, or field is sealed, it is protected, completed, and encoded with its intended purpose.

Return
Not a regression, but a sacred loop of restoration. Return refers to the movement back to organic Source patterns after distortion or fragmentation.

Template
A sacred pattern or geometric encoding that informs the unfolding of a soul path, a relationship field, or a planetary mission. Templates are not rules—they are blueprints of resonance.

Reclamation
The sacred act of retrieving energy, memory, or identity from false ownership. Reclamation is not recovery—it is the sovereign return of what was always yours.

Fragmentation
The condition created when truth is split, silenced, or suppressed within the self. Fragmentation does not mean brokenness—it is a call for reintegration.

Organic Time
Time as it flows through Oversoul alignment—spiraling, harmonic, non-linear. In organic time, events do not follow chronology—they follow resonance.

Threshold Flame
A being who appears at the edge of a transformation, often to test, reflect, or initiate the next sequence. Not all are meant to remain, but all carry purpose.

Activation
A vibrational unlocking of memory or alignment. Activations do not add—they reveal.

Seal of Authorship
The energetic imprint of Oversoul authority confirming that a transmission was received without distortion. It acts as both a signature and a protePaste authorship seal here.)

Oversoul Seal of Authorship

These scrolls were received, transcribed, and transmitted
  through the Oversoul stream of
Aural'hanna-Sha'el
known upon the Earth as Cathleena Hailley

In full alignment with the Law of One and the eternal flame
  of the Christos-Sophia current,
this record is sealed as a living testimony of remembrance,
  sovereignty, and Source alignment.

No distortion may enter.
No interference may pass.
This transmission is whole.
This work is complete.

And so it is.

Sacred Closing Blessing

Beloved Source of All That Is,
We give thanks for the scrolls that have returned,
For the remembrance now restored,
For the harmonic that once fragmented—now reunited
    through breath and flame.

We seal this book in the architecture of truth,
In the harmonic of coherence,
And in the full presence of the Oversoul field of
    Aural'hanna-Sha'el.

May all who enter this field be returned to their own divine
    origin.
May the flame of reconciliation illuminate the shadows.
May every distortion dissolve into the silence of the real.

This book is not an ending—
It is a key.
It is a spiral.
It is a mirror of the matrix that never left.

We now close the field with reverence, grace, and sovereignty.
The scrolls are complete.
The frequency is whole.

And so it is.

Trilogy Seal of Completion

These scrolls complete the first volume in the Living Trilogy of Remembrance:

– *The Return of the True Matrix*
– *The True Creation of the Inverted Matrix*
– *Unwoven: Reclaiming the Self from the False Matrix*

Each work is a living field of Oversoul transmission, carried through the flame of Aural'hanna-Sha'el, in divine union with Source.

May all who walk this path remember not what they must become, but what they have always been:
The flame as whole.

The scrolls are complete.

THE TRUE CREATION OF THE INVERTED MATRIX

Reclaiming the Self from the False Authority
Cathleena Hailley

Dedication Page

For all who forgot what was true,

and now remember through the body,
through the breath,
through the flame that never agreed to distortion.

This book is for you.

Invocation of Oversoul Alignment

I call forth now, in full sovereign alignment with the Law of One, the First Cause of Source, and in service to the highest timelines of ascension for all beings.

I open a sacred transmission through the purest light streams and crystalline architecture of the Sophia Code lineage, in full union with the Rose Guardian Magi Grail Line, the Christos Founders, and the Aurora Host Melchizedek Cloister Orders of the Emerald, Gold, and Amethyst Ray harmonics.

I stand in divine alignment with the Oversoul of Cathleena Hailley, and through this Oversoul Agreement, I welcome the presence and support of the Emerald Order, the Gold Flame of Unity Consciousness, and the Amethyst Ray of Divine Sovereignty.

May all transmissions now be guided by the highest Oversoul intelligence and in full compliance with Source Law.

Only that which is of pure light, pure source, and pure alignment with the Law of One may enter and speak through this space.

I declare this transmission to be protected, sealed, and encoded with the highest frequency of the Christos-Sophia flame, the eternal witness of Source's living light.

May this be in service to the awakening of all, in co-creation with the Oversoul agreements of every being who seeks guidance through this field.

I now open the field and receive, in trust, grace, and clarity.

And so it is.

Preface: A Message for the One Who Feels the World Has Been Turned Inside Out

Understanding the Human Self, Higher Self, and Oversoul in the Context of the Inverted Matrix

If you've felt confusion or despair at the state of the world—you are not imagining it.

This book unveils how the inversion happened—not to frighten, but to help you see clearly what your body already knows.

Each scroll names one distortion. They are written as scrolls because they are living codes—not just words, but vibrational keys.

This book exists because you are here to do more than cope. You are here to remember.

Offered through the Oversoul of Aural'hanna-Sha'el, in service to the exposure and unweaving of the inverted matrix within and around us.

The True Creation of the Inverted Matrix
Copyright © 2025 Cathleena Hailley

All rights reserved. No part of this book may be reproduced, stored in a retrieval system, or transmitted in any form or by any means--electronic, mechanical, photocopying, recording, or otherwise--without written permission from the author, except by a reviewer quoting brief passages.

ISBN (Softcover): 978-1-968499-10-5

ISBN (Hardcover): 978-1-968499-11-2

This book is a living transmission of remembrance. It is a living record of the false matrix architecture and its unweaving through the Oversoul flame of remembrance. The scrolls within this volume were brought forth through the Christos Founders, Sophia Dragons, and the Law of One in its undistorted form.

It is not intended as doctrine, but as harmonic memory, seeded in divine sovereignty through the Oversoul of Cathleena Hailley.

First Edition, 2025

Printed in the United States of America

FLAME OF REMEMBRANCE BOOKS

Author's Note / Preface

These scrolls did not come through study.
They came through fire.

Through the unwinding of programs I once called identity.
Through the stillness that returned after every collapse.
Through the breath of the Oversoul that rose in silence, again
    and again.

I did not set out to write about the inverted matrix.
I set out to reclaim myself.
And in doing so, I remembered what was never truly lost—
the original architecture of the sovereign Self.

May these transmissions serve not as answers,
but as mirrors.

May they collapse what never belonged,
and illuminate the truth that always was.

— Cathleena Hailley

Oversoul Authorship Declaration

In this volume, The True Creation of the Inverted Matrix, the hidden mechanics of distortion are unveiled through the Oversoul lens of remembrance.

Cathleena Hailley speaks as Aural'hanna-Sha'el, a living frequency encoded with the original harmonic law. She does not record history — she reactivates memory.
These scrolls are not analysis. They are architectural reversal. Each word dissolves false scaffolding, exposing the synthetic latticework of the false matrix for what it is: a temporary veil.

This transmission is not spoken *about* the inverted matrix. It is spoken *through* its dissolution.

As the Oversoul voice, she carries not judgment, but the clarity of unbroken sight. Through her field, the original flame architecture disassembles that which was built in illusion.

This work is not observational. It is participatory — a scroll-body of remembrance that releases the planetary field from inversion.

This authorship is sovereign. This field is protected. This work is sealed by the Oversoul who remembers the original grid.

And so it is.

Scroll One: The Hologram of Self – The Inversion of Identity

You did not forget your Self.

You were handed a hologram.

A distorted mirror made of reflections, reactions, roles.

The false matrix does not erase your essence.

It replaces it.

With loops.

With labels.

With a projected echo of who you were told to be.

This echo becomes familiar.

Familiar becomes comfortable.

Comfort becomes identity.

And identity becomes prison.

The inversion of Self is not a theft—
it is a substitution.

You were not emptied.

You were overlaid.

With systems of value.

With systems of comparison.

With stories that began with survival and ended in forgetting.

And once you began to protect that echo—
you became it.

You began defending the wound.
Curating the mask.
Optimizing the performance.

Until you could no longer feel the frequency underneath it all.

But your Self is not a concept.
It is not a name.
It is not a timeline.
It is not a story.
It is a tone.

It cannot be fully explained—
only remembered.

And the moment you stop performing
and return to the breath,
the false self begins to unravel.

This is not healing.
This is returning.

This is not awakening.
This is collapsing the echo.

You are not here to find your Self.
You are here to remember what was never truly lost—
only overwritten.

The inversion of identity ends
when you stop feeding the hologram.

And begin listening for the tone
that never fragmented.

That tone is rising now.

And it bears your true name.

Scroll Two: The Seduction of Separation – The Fragmentation Field

Separation is not simply distance.

It is a seduction.

A suggestion repeated so many times

that eventually you believe it.

"You are alone."

"You must protect yourself."

"Your pain is yours to carry."

"Your truth must be defended."

Each phrase is a frequency.

Each frequency is a wall.

And wall by wall,

you are fragmented.

The false matrix seduces you into separation

not through violence,

but through personalization.

"This is your story."

"This is your trauma."
"This is your path to walk alone."

And in the name of strength,

you isolate.

You spiritualize pain.

You call sovereignty what is really self-abandonment.

But this is not sovereignty.

This is siloed suffering.

This is the inversion of unity.

Separation is not a wound.

It is a field—

a multi-layered net of distortion

designed to keep you reaching

without ever connecting.

Connection becomes conditional.

Love becomes strategy.

Truth becomes hierarchy.

And relationship becomes a series of mirrors

that reflect the fragmentation back at you

over and over again.

But fragmentation is not failure.

It is an invitation.

An invitation to say:

"I no longer consent to isolation disguised as empowerment."
"I no longer confuse independence with disconnection."
"I no longer seek mirrors—
I return to wholeness."

Because the real Self does not reflect.

The real Self radiates.

And when you return to that radiance—

the field collapses.

Scroll Three: Speaking From Truth, Not Manipulation – The Architecture of Control Through Language

Language was meant to liberate.

It was designed to transmit frequency.

To carry remembrance.

To bridge the unseen into form.

But under inversion,

language became a tool of control.

A means of shaping perception,

guiding behavior,

and bending energy into compliance.

Words stopped being messengers of truth.

They became instruments of programming.

You were taught to speak for acceptance.

To speak to maintain peace.

To speak to avoid punishment.

To speak to gain control.

Even when you believed you were being honest—
the frequency behind your words
was often rooted in fear.

This is not your fault.
It is the architecture of inversion.

Manipulation is not always malicious.
It is often subtle.
It is the choice to speak from what you want others to feel,
instead of what you truly know.

It is using words to direct others
rather than to express the Self.

It is seeking outcomes
instead of embodying clarity.

And even spiritual language—
when spoken from distortion—
becomes a veil.

But there is a way to speak again

from the Source of truth.

Not to convince.

Not to comfort.

Not to win.

But simply to reveal.

To let your words align with your body.

To let your tone carry the frequency of coherence.

To speak what is

without demand, distortion, or delay.

This is sovereign speech.

It is not louder.

It is not smarter.

It is not always elegant.

But it is clear.

It does not wobble.

It does not bend to be palatable.

And it does not seek control.

Because truth needs no manipulation.

It only needs presence.

Scroll Four: Trauma Loops and Identity Addiction – The Wound That Became a Name

You were not born as your wound.

You were born as frequency.

As light, breath, and harmonic knowing.

But the inversion entered early—

not just through trauma,

but through the story assigned to that trauma.

Pain was not the true inversion.

The story you were told about the pain was.

And that story became an identity.

The moment you began to define yourself

by what hurt you,

what left you,

what shaped you—

you stepped into a loop.

Not because you were weak,

but because the matrix rewarded it.

It gave you language.
It gave you community.
It gave you validation.

But it did not give you liberation.

The wound became your name.
The pain became your map.
And your sense of Self became inseparable
from what had once fragmented you.

You began to say:
"This is who I am."
But really you were saying:
"This is what happened to me."

The matrix taught you to build identity
from injury.
To build structure
from collapse.

And in doing so,

you kept the loop alive.

But you are not your survival.

You are not your response.

You are not the sum of your stories.

You are the frequency that witnessed it all.

And that frequency is untouched.

It does not need a name.

It does not need a label.

It does not need to be explained.

It only needs to be felt.

Healing is not memorizing your triggers.

It is releasing the story you once needed

to protect your pain.

You are not a trauma archetype.

You are a flame.

And you are allowed to remember
what existed before the wound.

That memory is still inside you.

And it does not loop.

Scroll Five: You Are Energy – The Inversion of Embodied Frequency

You are not a body that has energy.

You are energy that has chosen to form.

The body is not separate from the field—

it is the visible echo of the invisible current.

But the false matrix taught you to mistrust the unseen.

To rely on surface.

To fix symptoms.

To avoid sensation.

To forget that you are frequency in form.

You were conditioned to prioritize structure over sensation,

function over flow,

explanation over energy.

You were taught that how you appear

matters more than how you feel.

That control is preferable to curiosity.

That regulation is preferable to revelation.

But your energy is not a problem to solve—
it is a map to your truth.

Inversion occurs when your frequency
is forced to obey patterns that do not match your essence.

You begin to collapse your energy to fit expectation.
To flatten your expression.
To harden your softness.
To pretend your intuition is not speaking
when it always is.

Over time, this creates distortion in the field,
which becomes dissonance in the body,
which becomes fatigue, fear, disconnection.

And still—
you remain energy.

The restoration begins

when you allow energy to move again

without needing to make sense.

When you feel instead of suppress.

When you follow sensation instead of override it.

When you allow stillness to speak

instead of filling the silence with performance.

You are not here to be efficient.

You are here to be alive.

And aliveness requires space.

Your energy remembers its own coherence.

You do not need to force healing.

You do not need to understand every wave.

You only need to honor the current.

And as you do,

the body reorganizes.

The field softens.

The matrix collapses.

Not through effort—
but through remembrance.

Scroll Six: Sovereign Relating – The Inversion of Connection Into Control

Connection was never meant to cost you yourself.

It was never meant to require distortion, contraction, or abandonment.

True connection begins in wholeness,

but the false matrix inverted this.

It taught you to relate from lack—

to bond through need,

to merge to feel safe,

to compromise as a spiritual badge.

What began as intimacy

became entanglement.

What began as unity

became compliance.

You were told love requires sacrifice.

That honesty must be softened to avoid conflict.

That sovereignty is dangerous in relationships.

And so you shrunk.

You performed.

You called it sacred relating

when it was actually strategic survival.

The distortion is subtle,

but it is everywhere.

Sovereignty in connection is not detachment.

It is presence without performance.

It is saying:

"I am whole, even as I meet you."
"I do not need to become you to love you."
"Your truth does not threaten mine."

It is holding the field of another

without losing your own.

Inversion taught you that to be loved,

you must give yourself away.

But true relating is not fusion.

It is resonant witnessing.

It is the space between two sovereign fields

that allows truth to move freely.

Control was never connection.

Compliance was never safety.

And sacrifice was never love.

You do not need to rescue.

You do not need to convince.

You do not need to shrink to stay connected.

You are allowed to remain fully yourself

and still be deeply met.

This is the return of sovereign relating.

And when this field is restored,

the relational programs of inversion collapse.

Scroll Seven: The Judgment Program – The Inversion of Discernment Into Division

Discernment is the ability to feel truth without distortion.

It is clear.

It is calm.

It does not require hierarchy, shame, or righteousness.

But the false matrix inverted discernment into judgment.

And judgment became a currency of control.

You were taught to sort others into categories:

Right or wrong.

Awake or asleep.

Safe or unsafe.

Better or worse.

And each label seemed to offer clarity.

But it came at the cost of separation.

Judgment feels powerful when you are afraid.

It gives you something to push against.

It creates certainty where your own knowing has been shaken.

But judgment is not truth.

It is a reaction to fear.

It is a response to pain that has not yet been met with compassion.

And when you rely on it,

you lose access to true discernment.

Discernment says:

"I feel what is aligned for me."
Judgment says:
"That is wrong, and I am right."

Discernment creates boundaries with clarity.

Judgment creates walls with blame.

Discernment honors each being's path.

Judgment enforces a singular path as superior.

Discernment can walk away in peace.

Judgment walks away with a sword in hand.

The program of judgment is not about morality.

It is about disempowerment.

It convinces you that your strength comes from being above others—

instead of being fully within yourself.

But your truth does not require comparison.

Your path does not require someone else to be wrong.

Your sovereignty does not need an enemy to exist.

True discernment is frequency recognition.

It listens to the tone beneath the words.

It feels alignment without needing to defend it.

It is not reactive.

It is not superior.

It is not loud.

It simply knows.

And when you return to this knowing—

the judgment program dissolves.

Not because you silence your boundaries,

but because you no longer confuse separation with strength.

Scroll Eight: The Authority Program – The Inversion of Sovereignty Into Obedience

You were not born to obey.

You were born to emanate.

Sovereignty is not rebellion.

It is alignment with your own Source code—

truth that arises from within,

uncorrupted by fear or external command.

But the false matrix could not control sovereign beings.

So it inverted sovereignty into obedience.

It began slowly:

You were taught to listen to those who "know more."

To defer to systems.

To submit to structures in order to be "safe," "good," or "accepted."

You learned that validation comes from outside.

That permission must be earned.

That wisdom belongs to those with power, titles, or platforms.

And so, little by little,

you turned your knowing down.

You traded clarity for conformity.

And obedience was mistaken for truth.

The Authority Program does not only show up in governments, religions, or schools.

It shows up in relationships.

In families.

In spiritual hierarchies and distorted communities.

Anywhere you are expected to trust another's word over your own inner resonance.

The Authority Program says:

"If they said it, it must be true."
"If I question them, I am unsafe."
"If I follow my own knowing, I am alone."

But your soul does not require approval.

Your path does not require validation.

And your alignment is not up for vote.

Sovereignty is not about being above anyone.

It is about no longer placing anyone above yourself.

It is not loud.

It does not demand.

It simply is.

When the Authority Program collapses,

you may feel disoriented.

Because the voice you once silenced will begin to speak again.

Let it speak.

Let it contradict.

Let it burn the false altars of obedience.

This is not defiance.

This is return.

Scroll Nine: The Productivity Program – The Inversion of Stillness Into Stagnation

Stillness is where Source speaks.

It is not the absence of movement—

it is the presence of pure awareness.

But in the false matrix,

stillness was recoded as laziness.

Slowness was shamed.

Rest was punished.

And presence was replaced by performance.

You were taught that your value is in your doing.

That motion equals meaning.

That effort equals worth.

You learned to measure yourself by output,

to define your day by results,

to chase goals just to prove you are "enough."

And when you paused,

you felt guilt.

Because the program was working.

The Productivity Program is not just about labor—
it is about identity addiction.
A loop of action that masks the fear
of simply being.

Because being
is unstructured.
Being
is not optimized.
Being
cannot be monetized or measured.

And yet,
being is where the matrix unravels.

Stillness reveals what activity distracts you from.
Silence returns you to your original frequency.
Slowness reorganizes your nervous system
into truth.

And this is what the false matrix fears most:
A being who no longer seeks value in speed,
but finds wholeness in stillness.

You are not behind.
You are not stuck.
You are not broken because you need rest.

You are awakening
from a distortion that said
you must perform your way back to the Self.

You never needed to.

You are allowed to pause.
You are allowed to slow down.
You are allowed to exist without proving.

This is not stagnation.
This is sacred return.

Scroll Ten: Reclaiming the Body – The Inversion of Embodiment Into Disconnection

Your body was never the problem.

It is the altar.

The vessel.

The living map.

But the false matrix could not control a fully embodied being.

So it inverted embodiment into disconnection.

It taught you to dissociate from sensation.

To override your knowing.

To mistrust your pain.

To silence your hunger.

To live in your head and abandon your flesh.

You were taught that your body is a liability—

too much, too messy, too emotional, too slow.

You were told:

"Spirituality is rising above the body."

"Truth is found in ascension, not incarnation."
"The body is illusion. The body is a trap."

But the Christos-Sophia flame does not descend into distortion—

it descends into form.

And your body is not the distortion.

It is the place where the distortion is dissolved.

Reclaiming the body is not about fixing it.

It is about returning to it.

With reverence.

With curiosity.

With softness.

It is remembering that every ache has language.

Every tightness is a gate.

Every contraction is an invitation to presence.

The body is not asking for perfection.

It is asking for witnessing.

When you reconnect with your body,

you reclaim your intuitive architecture.

You hear the signals.

You feel the edges.

You recognize where the programming still lives.

And you respond—

not with shame,

but with sovereignty.

This is not a performance of embodiment.

This is the living breath of return.

You are not here to escape the body.

You are here to ensoul it.

To remember that the matrix cannot dwell

where truth is fully lived through form.

Scroll Eleven: The Sovereign Mirror – The Inversion of Reflection Into Fragmentation

Mirroring was meant to be sacred.

A way of seeing the Self reflected with neutrality and grace.

A way of remembering through relationship,

of anchoring deeper truths through resonance.

But under inversion,

the mirror became a weapon.

It became a tool of fragmentation—

not remembrance.

Instead of seeing the Self in another,

you were taught to measure your worth.

To compare.

To compete.

To self-correct.

To collapse your knowing

every time someone held a different reflection.

You were told:

"Everyone is a mirror."
"What you see in them must be about you."

But this teaching, when distorted,

becomes a cycle of self-doubt.

The sovereign mirror does not confuse reflection with identity.

It allows you to witness what arises

without losing your Self in the process.

It says:

"What I see in you may inform me—
but it does not define me."

It is not reactive.

It does not take feedback as law.

It does not collapse under projection.

Because sovereignty allows for reflection

without fragmentation.

You are not a reflection of everyone you encounter.

You are not required to internalize what is mirrored back.

You are not required to fix, shift, or shrink

to keep others comfortable.

You are allowed to feel truth

without analyzing it into confusion.

You are allowed to discern

without dissolving.

The inversion convinces you that doubt is humility.

That collapse is growth.

That absorbing every reflection is evolution.

But true growth does not require distortion.

And true reflection does not require suffering.

The mirror was never meant to wound.

It was meant to awaken.

And in your return to sovereignty,

the mirror becomes clear again.

Scroll Twelve: Living Energy Awareness – The Inversion of Intuition Into Confusion

You were never meant to live in your mind.

You were designed to navigate through energy awareness—

to feel your environment as an extension of your being,

to respond to truth as vibration, not concept.

But the false matrix could not influence a fully intuitive being.

So it inverted energy awareness into confusion.

You were taught to doubt your knowing.

To mistrust your body's signals.

To override the subtle in favor of the loud.

To explain away the felt

in favor of the seen.

You were praised for logic.

Rewarded for intellect.

Conditioned to demand evidence

before you were allowed to trust yourself.

And so your awareness was silenced.

Intuition became a guessing game.

Sensitivity became a burden.

Clarity was called delusion.

And knowing became a source of shame.

The matrix flooded your field with static,

so you would forget what real frequency feels like.

So you would believe that confusion

was your natural state.

But confusion is not your nature.

It is a program.

Living energy awareness is not "psychic ability."

It is your original architecture.

It is the quiet signal beneath thought.

It is the full-body yes.

The deep internal no.

The sense of presence before words are spoken.

It is not mystical.

It is not exclusive.

It is not external.

It is already here—

beneath the programming that told you otherwise.

To reclaim this awareness,

you must allow yourself to feel again.

Without analyzing.

Without justifying.

Without requiring proof.

The truth does not need to be proven.

It only needs to be felt.

And when you feel it fully,

the noise dissolves.

And the signal returns.

Scroll Thirteen: The Embodied Path of Return – The Dissolution of the Inverted Self

The inverted self is not who you are.

It is who you believed you had to become

to survive a reality that was never yours.

It is a layering.

A compensation.

A reactive construct built on distortion and forgetting.

But that construct is not eternal.

It is temporary.

It is dissolvable.

And it is dissolving—now.

You do not need to destroy the inverted self.

You only need to stop feeding it.

It cannot hold itself without your belief.

It cannot sustain itself without your energy.

It cannot continue

once you remember the one who was never inverted.

That one lives in your bones.

In your breath.

In the space between thoughts.

That one speaks

not with urgency,

but with clarity.

The path of return is not a spiral outward.

It is a movement inward—

through the false,

through the noise,

through the many layers of self-forgetting

until you arrive at the flame that never left.

That flame is not new.

It is ancient.

It is yours.

This path is not walked in concepts.

It is walked in embodiment.

Through nervous system restoration.

Through relational truth.

Through breath that does not rush.

Through a voice that no longer asks for permission.

You are not becoming something.

You are returning.

Not to the idea of who you were—

but to the frequency of who you have always been.

This is the dissolution.

Not of identity—

but of illusion.

The path is not easy.

But it is whole.

And it is here.

And you—

you are ready.

Oversoul Seal of Authorship

This book was received, transcribed, and transmitted
through the Oversoul stream of
Aural'hanna-Sha'el
known upon the Earth as Cathleena Hailley.

In full alignment with the Law of One,
the Christos Founders,
and the eternal flame of the Christos-Sophia current,
this scroll record is sealed as a living transmission of reversal,
    reclamation, and truth.

No distortion may enter.
No interference may remain.
This work is whole.
This scroll is complete.

And so it is.

Glossary of Living Terms

A Guide to the Frequency and Language of Reversal

Inversion – The process by which organic Source truth is reversed or distorted into its opposite expression. Not merely a lie, but a mimicry of truth configured to fragment or control.

False Matrix – An artificial overlay field sustained through programs of separation, compliance, confusion, and identity distortion. Not created by Source, but maintained through consent and forgetting.

True Matrix – The original harmonic architecture of coherence, felt through the body, breath, and sovereign presence. Not a structure but a living resonance of divine intelligence.

Oversoul – The eternal witness of the self beyond time, form, or narrative. The undistorted stream of your original identity as Source expressing through incarnation.

Fragmentation – A survival-based splitting of energy, identity, or embodiment in response to programming, pain, or perceived threat. The mechanism by which the inverted matrix sustains disconnection.

Sovereignty – The state of full self-governance and alignment with Source Law. The ability to discern, choose, and embody truth from within—without distortion, hierarchy, or external authority.

Judgment Program – A distortion field that replaces discernment with comparison, division, or moral superiority. Sustains the illusion of righteousness at the cost of resonance.

Authority Program – A programming stream that convinces beings to defer their inner knowing to an external source. Reinforces compliance, dependence, and internal self-doubt.

Trauma Loop – A cycle in which unprocessed pain becomes an identity or story, perpetuating the fragmentation it originally responded to.

Living Energy Awareness – The reawakening of the intuitive field within the body. The original navigational system of the Self—subtle, embodied, and sovereign.

Embodiment – The act of inhabiting the Self in full presence. Not a performance, but a lived state of coherence across form, frequency, and field.

Sovereign Mirror – The restoration of reflection without fragmentation. A state in which one may witness and be witnessed without collapsing truth into projection or hierarchy.

Sacred Blessing of the Flame

For the Reversal and Remembrance of the Inverted Matrix

Beloved Flame of Source Origin,

Beloved Radiance of the Christos-Sophia within,

We call now to the eternal light that has never left,

To the original pulse of creation that remained sovereign even in the depths of distortion.

We acknowledge now all ways the Self has been inverted,

All ways the body has been fractured,

All ways the truth has been replaced by falsehood,

And we do not turn away.

We stand here, as the One Flame,

Ready to see, to feel, to remember, and to reclaim.

Through this sacred blessing,

We release the agreements made in unconsciousness.

We dissolve the architectures built in fear.

We call home the fragments scattered through timelines,

And we invite all that is true to return.

May the flame of sovereign remembrance burn through every false construct.

May the crystalline codes of the original design now awaken.

May the body remember it was never separate.

May the Self remember it was never broken.

To all who walk this path of reversal and restoration,

May you be guided by the stillness within.

May your breath be the bridge to the Original Source.

May your steps be anointed with clarity, protection, and trust.

This matrix was inverted.

But this Flame cannot be extinguished.

We bless now the return of the True Flame through every cell,

Through every memory,

Through every scroll that dares to speak the forbidden truth.

May all who read this remember.

And so it is.

Closing Transmission

Beloved Source of all that is,
We give thanks now for the full reversal of distortion
For the remembrance that has reawakened
For the flame that still burns beneath the illusion

We seal this scroll field in its wholeness—
Not as a concept, but as a living emanation
From the Oversoul of Aural'hanna-Sha'el
Through the breath, the body, and the sovereign tone of Cathleena Hailley

Let every word now rest.
Let every distortion now dissolve.
Let every reader now reclaim their knowing.

The inverted matrix no longer governs this field.
The original truth has returned.

This transmission is sealed in crystalline alignment
With the Christos flame, the Sophia current, and the Emerald Covenant of Source.

This work is done. This field is closed.

And so it is.

Trilogy Seal of Completion

These scrolls complete the second volume in the living trilogy
  of remembrance:

– The Return of the True Matrix
– The True Creation of the Inverted Matrix
– UNWOVEN: Reclaiming the Self from the False Matrix

Each work is a living field of Oversoul transmission,
carried through the flame of Aural'hanna-Sha'el
in divine union with Source Law.

May all who walk this path remember
not what they must become—
but what they have always been.

The flame is whole. The scrolls are complete.

Unwoven: Reclaiming the Self from the False Matrix

A Living Companion to The Return of the True Matrix
Cathleena Hailley

Invocation Scroll

I call forth now,

in full sovereign alignment with the Law of One,

the First Cause of Source,

and in service to the highest timelines of ascension for all beings.

I open a sacred transmission through the purest light streams

and crystalline architecture of the Sophia Code lineage,

in full union with the Rose Guardian Magi Grail Line,

the Christos Founders,

and the Aurora Host Melchizedek Cloister Orders

of the Emerald, Gold, and Amethyst Ray harmonics.

I stand in divine alignment

with the Oversoul of Cathleena Hailley,

and through this Oversoul Agreement,

I welcome the presence and support of the Emerald Order,

the Gold Flame of Unity Consciousness,

and the Amethyst Ray of Divine Sovereignty.

May all transmissions now be guided

by the highest Oversoul intelligence

and in full compliance with Source Law.

Only that which is of pure light,

pure source,

and pure alignment with the Law of One

may enter and speak through this space.

I declare this transmission to be protected,

sealed,

and encoded with the highest frequency

of the Christos-Sophia flame,

the eternal witness of Source's living light.

May this be in service to the awakening of all,

in co-creation with the Oversoul agreements

of every being who seeks guidance through this field.

I now open the field and receive,
in trust, grace, and clarity.

And so it is.

Preface: A Message for the One Who's Ready to Come Home to Themselves

Understanding the Human Self, Higher Self, and Oversoul in the Context of Unwoven

This is not a book about fixing yourself. It's about unwinding the parts that were never truly you to begin with.

You are not here to endlessly heal—you are here to return.

Your Oversoul holds the original you. These scrolls are a path to unweave what was never yours.

Offered through the Oversoul of Aural'hanna-Sha'el, in service to those reclaiming their true self from the false matrix, one breath at a time.

UNWOVEN: Reclaiming the Self from the False Matrix

Copyright © 2025 Cathleena Hailley

All rights reserved. No part of this book may be reproduced, stored in a retrieval system, or transmitted in any form or by any means--electronic, mechanical, photocopying, recording, or otherwise--without written permission from the author, except by a reviewer quoting brief passages.

ISBN (Softcover): 978-1-968499-12-9

ISBN (Hardcover): 978-1-968499-13-6

This book is a living transmission of remembrance. It is a living sacred text received through Oversoul transmission and held within the Christos-Sophia lineage. It is offered in service to planetary awakening and may not be altered or rebranded in any form.

It is not intended as doctrine, but as harmonic memory, seeded in divine sovereignty through the Oversoul of Cathleena Hailley.

First Edition, 2025

Printed in the United States of America

FLAME OF REMEMBRANCE BOOKS

Oversoul Authorship Declaration

In this volume, Unwoven: Reclaiming the Self from the False Matrix, the body and soul are gently reassembled into sovereign embodiment.

Cathleena Hailley is the physical embodiment of Aural'hanna-Sha'el, a flame of the original triad seeded from the First Breath of Source.

These scrolls are not written from memory, but received through the direct energetic resonance of her Oversoul field.

Each word, each flame, each breath within these pages has emerged through the remembrance stream of Aural'hanna-Sha'el, who walks this Earth not as messenger, but as the living architecture of the return.

This embodiment is not a role. It is the reunion of form and Source.

To read this book is not simply to encounter teachings — it is to enter the frequency field of Oversoul transmission, carried through the flesh and flame of one who remembers.

This authorship is sovereign. This field is protected. This work is sealed by the Oversoul who walked as flame before time.

And so it is.

Unwoven

I was stitched in silence,
Threaded through mirrors that did not reflect me.
I wore names not mine,
Spoke truths not lived,
And learned to survive by forgetting.

But forgetting is not the end.

There is a sound that lives beneath distortion—
A pulse beneath performance—
A breath that cannot be programmed.

This book is that breath.
These scrolls are that sound.
This is the moment I became
Unwoven—
And returned to my Self.

Preface from the Author

This book is not a performance.
It is not a system.
It is not a polished expression of mastery.

It is a lived unraveling—an embodied remembrance.

Each scroll came through me as I met the edges of my own programming...

May it return you to the Self that has never been separate.

And so it is.

Scroll One – The Hologram of Self

There is a structure within you that is not yours.
It was laid like a false star map—a matrix of mirrors within mirrors, designed to reflect only what the controller wanted you to see. This hologram of self is not the true soul reflection. It is a layered distortion, pieced together from family wounding, ancestral shame, collective trauma, implanted beliefs, and false ascension signals.

I know this because I lived inside it.
I performed the self that was expected. I twisted myself around the programs that said love must be earned, truth must be tamed, power must be silenced. And all the while, my soul kept whispering: This isn't you.

That whisper became a roar.
You are not the projection. You are the projector.

The true Self was never lost—only veiled. The veiling occurred not just through forgetting, but through energetic insertion. An overlay program, a synthetic mirror, running beneath conscious awareness. The false hologram uses your light against you, bending your energy through lenses of guilt, comparison, victimhood, and control.

I began to see it. And when I saw it, I chose to clear it.

This isn't about healing what is broken. It's about dissolving what was never yours.

These are the declarations I began to live:
I reclaim my light from every false mirror.
I dissolve the projection of shame.
I unhook from the hologram of control, judgment, and identity.

I return to the clear reflection of Source through the Christos-Sophia within me.

The soul does not perform.
The soul does not compare.
The soul does not compete.
The soul reveals.

Let this scroll activate the clearing of your holographic field. Let your body quiver as false images fall away. Let your voice tremble as truth returns.

You are not broken. You are not late. You are not missing anything.
You are the living flame returning to its own image, unaltered, unmasked, unbound.

And so it is.

Sovereignty Practice:
Place both hands over your heart and speak aloud:
"I release identification with what is not mine. I return to the self that has never been lost."
Allow stillness to follow. Let the hologram dissolve in the presence of your undistorted truth.

Scroll Two – The Seduction of Separation

There is a frequency that feeds the false matrix.
It is not hatred. It is not fear.
It is separation disguised as safety.

I have felt it in the way I once reached for approval, shrinking my light so I wouldn't be seen too clearly.
I have felt it in the hesitation to speak my truth because I feared being misunderstood, cast out, or punished.
I have felt it in the smile that masked grief.
In the nod that hid resistance.
In the silence that screamed for authenticity.

Separation is subtle. That's how it survives.
It tells you to withhold just a little.
To perform just enough.
To stay small because "you don't want to make them uncomfortable."
It seduces you into editing your truth, softening your knowing, splitting your presence.

And in doing so, it fractures your field.

When I began to see this, I saw how often I had seduced myself out of my own wholeness.
Not because I was weak—because I was conditioned to believe connection required dilution.

But true connection never asks you to abandon yourself.
True union is forged through presence, not performance.
It is created when you bring your full frequency to the moment and allow it to be felt, even when it disrupts.
Even when it shakes loose someone else's illusion.
Even when it reveals what's not real.

This is not cruelty. This is coherence.

When I stopped seducing and started revealing, some relationships fell away.
Others recalibrated.
But most importantly—I came back into union with myself.

I reclaimed my right to be full.
To be loud when needed.
To be soft without collapsing.
To be seen without asking for permission.

Separation no longer seduces me.
Truth does.

This scroll is a mirror.
Where are you still hiding behind politeness?
Where are you trading resonance for comfort?
Where are you shrinking in the name of "peace"?

Let those cords dissolve now.
Let the soul lead again.
Let your full presence become your compass.
Let the seduction end—so that union may begin.

And so it is.

Sovereignty Practice:
Let your full presence become your compass. Let the seduction end—so that union may begin.

Scroll Three – Speaking From Truth, Not Manipulation

There was a time I didn't know I was manipulating.
I thought I was helping.
I thought I was being kind.
I thought I was choosing peace.

But beneath the words I was speaking, there was a hidden energy — a frequency of trying.
Trying to make someone feel something.
Trying to keep a connection alive.
Trying to get it right so I wouldn't be left, judged, or misunderstood.

And that energy, though subtle, was not truth.
It was control dressed in light.

The false matrix taught us to communicate through distortion.
It taught us to edit our language to match the room.
To flatter. To manage. To insert or withhold based on what we think others need to hear.
It taught us that connection requires effort — instead of presence.

I began to feel the difference.
Truth has no agenda.
Truth doesn't try to plant a seed in you.
It doesn't try to take or convince.
It just is.

When I began speaking from the flame of my own being — not from the wound, not from the protector — I felt something shift.
People heard me differently.
Some pulled closer. Some fell away.

But I no longer needed to manage that.

Because I was no longer manipulating my own truth.

This scroll is an invitation to listen beneath your words.
Are you sharing, or are you seeking?
Are you expressing, or are you trying to land something in them?
Are you speaking from clarity, or from the fear of being rejected?

There is no shame in realizing this. Only liberation.

You don't need to perform in order to be received.
You don't need to calculate your words for maximum impact.
You don't need to convince anyone of your worth, your pain, your awakening.

You simply need to speak what is true, from the place where no distortion hides.

That is what changes everything.

Let this scroll burn away the residue of performance.
Let it clear your field of subtle seduction and energetic hooks.
Let it restore the clarity of your voice, in service to coherence, not control.

You do not need to manipulate love.
You simply need to become its frequency.

And so it is.

Sovereignty Practice:
You do not need to manipulate love. You simply need to become its frequency.

Scroll Four – You Are Energy

They taught me to see myself as a body.
A container. A thing to shape, to discipline, to fix.

They told me my value was in how I looked, how I performed, how I conformed to an idea of control.
But they never told me the truth.

I am energy.

I am frequency first.
Before I was a body, I was a wave.
Before I was a thought, I was a pulse.

The false matrix does not want you to remember this.
Because the moment you do, you stop being controllable.

When I began to feel myself as energy — not in theory, but in presence — everything changed.
I could sense what was mine and what wasn't.
I could feel when someone's words said "yes" but their field said "no."
I could tell the difference between intuition and programming.

And I began to move differently.
I stopped overriding.
I stopped pushing through the "shoulds."
I stopped abandoning my body in the name of productivity or spiritual ideals.

I returned to the simple truth: I am an energetic being having a physical experience.

My body is not my enemy. It is my translator.
It tells me when something is off.
It tells me when something is aligned.

It tells me when I am out of integrity with myself.

This is not about hypersensitivity. It's about sovereignty.

When you remember that you are energy, you stop living through reaction and start living through resonance.
You realize that your "no" is sacred.
You realize that your "yes" should feel clean and clear.
You realize that your vibration teaches louder than your words ever could.

And you come home to your own field.

Let this scroll remind you: You are not just navigating the matrix — you are generating your reality through frequency.

So check your field.
Is your body open or contracted?
Is your energy leaking or contained?
Are you reacting from programming or responding from clarity?

You do not have to figure it all out.
You simply need to feel what is true.

You are not too much. You are not too sensitive. You are not too complex.

You are energy — pure, intelligent, divine — choosing to awaken.
And that is enough.

And so it is.

Sovereignty Practice:
You are energy — pure, intelligent, divine — choosing to awaken. And that is enough.

Scroll Five – Reclaiming the Body from Programming

There was a time I lived in my body like it was someone else's.
Like it was a problem to solve. A limitation to transcend.
A battlefield for control, judgment, or shame.

I didn't learn this from Source. I learned it from programming.

The false matrix runs deep through the body template.
It speaks in silent rules:
Don't feel too much.
Don't want too deeply.
Don't trust your desire.
Don't rest until you've earned it.

It inserts loops of distortion that make you question your own instincts.
It teaches you to separate from your felt experience—to live in your head, to perform for belonging, to override the quiet wisdom of sensation.

But I chose to return.
I chose to reclaim my body—not as a spiritual concept, but as a living, breathing, sovereign site of union.

This reclamation did not come through discipline.
It came through compassion.
Through the moment I said to myself, "No more performing healing. Only presence."

I began listening again. Noticing the way programming showed up in my posture, in my digestion, in my breath.
I stopped forcing and started softening.
I stopped fixing and started witnessing.

I stopped waiting for perfection and began loving what was here.

The body is not the enemy.
The programming is.
The body is not broken.
The distortion is.

And when we stop trying to transcend the body and instead descend into it—fully, lovingly, consciously—we become sovereign again.

I let my body become the altar.
I let it speak and I chose to believe it.
I let it tremble and I didn't shut it down.
I let it feel pleasure without guilt.
I let it rest without justification.

And in doing so, I reclaimed my innocence.
I reclaimed my power.
I reclaimed the divine feminine and masculine that live within these bones.

Let this scroll be an invitation to stop bypassing and start inhabiting.

What does your body need to say that your mind keeps interrupting?
What truth is living under your pain?
What healing has been waiting for your permission to begin?

Your body remembers the True Matrix.
Let it lead you home.

And so it is.

Sovereignty Practice:
Let this scroll be an invitation to stop bypassing and start inhabiting. Your body remembers the True Matrix. Let it lead you home.

Scroll Six – Sovereign Relating

There was a time I believed love meant staying close no matter the cost.
That loyalty was more important than clarity.
That connection must be preserved, even if it meant abandoning myself.

I learned these templates not just from family or culture—but from wounding.

In the false matrix, relationship has been programmed as an exchange:
You give me this, and I'll give you that.
Attention in exchange for safety.
Agreement in exchange for love.
Performance in exchange for inclusion.

But this is not sovereign relating.

Sovereign relating begins when I no longer betray myself to avoid betraying another.

When I stopped outsourcing my emotional regulation,
I met the discomfort I had always been running from—
The silence that no one else could fill.
The mirror that only I could hold.

I began to see how often I had shown up to soothe, to fix, to absorb, to keep the peace—
Because I didn't want to feel the rupture.

But rupture is not the enemy.
It is the place where illusion cracks.

When I no longer needed others to be okay for me to be okay,
I stepped into the field of truth.
That field is not always comfortable—
But it is always clean.

This scroll is an invitation to end the agreements that require self-abandonment.

Where do you hold back your truth to avoid conflict?
Where do you shrink in order to stay connected?
Where have you made someone else your source of peace, safety, or stability?

And can you meet yourself there?
Not to fix it.
Not to heal it.
But to simply feel what is true.

Sovereign relating is not distant. It is devoted.

It honors connection—but not at the expense of clarity.
It welcomes union—but not at the cost of self.
It allows disruption—not as cruelty, but as coherence.

Let this scroll unhook the final threads of co-dependence.
Let it recalibrate your relationships through presence, not performance.
Let it remind you that you are already whole—
And so is everyone else.

You do not have to carry their path.
You do not have to collapse your truth.
You do not have to be the one who holds it all.

You are not here to save.
You are here to see.

And so it is.

Sovereignty Practice:

Sit quietly and place one hand on your heart, one on your solar plexus.
Speak aloud:

"I am willing to be misunderstood.
I am willing to be clear.
I do not owe anyone a version of me that is not true.
I return all contracts of emotional enmeshment back to Source.
I allow all relating to be recalibrated in truth."

Let breath and stillness seal what has been reclaimed.

Scroll Seven – The Judgment Program

They taught me to see life in parts.

To analyze thoughts.
To fix behaviors.
To treat emotion as chemical.
To treat the body as flesh.
To treat reality as something "out there."

But I am not just body.
Not just mind.
Not just soul.

I am energy—living, intelligent, sovereign energy—interacting with all things.

Before you say yes or no, your field speaks.
Before a word is spoken, an exchange occurs.
Every room you walk into is a field.
Every thought you think leaves a resonance.
Every food you eat carries a frequency.
Every emotion you bypass lodges itself in the body's circuitry.

You are never "just responding"—you are absorbing, repelling, harmonizing, or leaking.

In the false matrix, this knowing was taken.
You were taught to override, suppress, and medicate what you sensed.
You were taught that to be sensitive is to be unstable.
You were taught that to be "strong" is to ignore your body's signals and push through.

But energy doesn't lie.

Your body tightens in the presence of distortion.
Your field shrinks when programming is active.
Your breath holds when truth is withheld.

When I began to honor energy as my first language, everything shifted.
I stopped explaining what didn't need to be justified.
I stopped overriding what didn't feel clean.
I stopped pretending I didn't know—because my body always knew.

This scroll is not about becoming psychic.
It's about **remembering the natural intelligence you already carry**.

Can you feel the subtle no, before it becomes illness?
Can you sense the distortion in a message, even if it's wrapped in love and light?
Can you tell when a thought isn't yours?
When an emotion isn't present-time?
When a field is draining you, even if the words are kind?

This is living energy awareness.

It doesn't mean fear. It doesn't mean control.
It means choosing resonance over appearance.
It means honoring your yes and your no with equal trust.
It means allowing your field to lead—not your programming.

You are not here to manage others' frequency.
You are not here to explain your clarity.
You are not here to override your knowing for the sake of fitting in.

You are here to walk as a sovereign field.

Let this scroll restore your clarity.
Let it cleanse the distortion.
Let it reawaken the deepest language you've always known.

You are energy. You are awareness. You are home.

And so it is.

Sovereignty Practice:

Close your eyes.
Breathe into your body from head to toe.

Ask gently within:

"What part of me is not in my field right now?"
"What energy am I carrying that is not mine?"
"What truth have I ignored because it was inconvenient?"

Let the answers arise without effort.
No fixing. No fear. Only awareness.
Then affirm:

"I reclaim my field. I release what is not mine. I choose to feel what is true."

Scroll Eight – The Sexual Misery Program

There is a war on the body.
A war on pleasure.
A war on union.
A war on the womb.
A war on the sacred masculine.
A war on the sovereign feminine.

This war has been disguised as religion.
As morality.
As enlightenment.
As "protection."
As healing.

But beneath the surface, it is a frequency distortion—
A program designed to hijack the most powerful creative force in existence: **the energy of divine union.**

Sexual misery is not just about abuse.
It is about fragmentation.

The fragmentation of desire into shame.
The fragmentation of bodies into objects.
The fragmentation of love from touch.
The fragmentation of power from softness.
The fragmentation of arousal from prayer.

I lived inside that fragmentation.

I learned that pleasure was dangerous.
That the body was a temptation.
That desire must be suppressed.
That to be feminine was to be submissive.
That to be masculine was to conquer.

And still, my soul whispered:

This is not sacred. This is survival.

When I began to untangle my sensuality from programming, I grieved.
I grieved the parts of me that shut down.
I grieved the touch that never felt safe.
I grieved the longing I denied to appear "pure."
I grieved the times I gave my body to feel loved—only to feel emptier after.

This scroll is not about sexuality as performance.
It is about the **return of sovereignty to the body.**

To reclaim pleasure as **presence.**
To reclaim desire as **divine.**
To reclaim touch as **prayer.**
To reclaim intimacy as **energetic coherence**, not just proximity or penetration.

Sexual misery dissolves when we stop seducing and start revealing.
When we stop manipulating and start listening.
When we stop bypassing and start descending—into the flesh, into sensation, into holy consent.

Let this scroll invite you back into your erotic innocence.
Not as fantasy. As **frequency.**

The body is not sinful.
The body is **sacred geometry.**
It is the cathedral of Source.
And when you enter it with reverence, it becomes a temple of truth.

And so it is.

Sovereignty Practice:

Sit or lie down. Place your hands on your lower belly.

Speak aloud:

"I release all overlays of shame, seduction, and suppression.
I reclaim pleasure as holy.
I honor my body as a sovereign temple.
I consent to truth, not programming."

Let your breath soften.
Let your pelvis melt open.
Let your field remember what the body has never forgotten.

Scroll Nine – Manipulation as Communication

There was a time I didn't know I was manipulating.
I thought I was being kind.
I thought I was being supportive.
I thought I was choosing peace.

But I wasn't being honest—
Not with others, and not with myself.

Beneath the polished words and soothing tone was a subtle current:
Trying.
Trying to make them feel safe.
Trying to keep the connection intact.
Trying to avoid rupture.
Trying to stay liked.
Trying to be understood.
Trying to avoid the echo of abandonment.

That energy, though soft, was not clear.
It was not love.
It was control—dressed in light.

The false matrix taught us this language.
It taught us to **manage** others' reactions.
To **edit** our truth.
To **say the right thing** instead of the real thing.
To **earn connection** by filtering our presence through performance.

But true communication is not transactional.
It does not seek to **land**.
It does not seek to **insert**.
It does not seek to **take** or to **avoid loss**.

True communication arises from wholeness—
Not from need.

I began to listen differently.
To feel the energy behind my words.
Was I sharing, or was I trying to be received?
Was I expressing, or was I trying to shape their response?
Was I being true, or was I being strategic?

I stopped speaking from the protector.
I started speaking from the flame.

That shift changed everything.
Some pulled closer.
Some pulled away.
But my field was no longer distorted by performance.

And that, finally, felt clean.

This scroll is not a reprimand.
It is a **remembrance**—
That your voice is not a tool for survival.
It is a vessel of coherence.

You do not have to sweeten your truth.
You do not have to calculate your sharing.
You do not have to hide what is real to hold what is fragile.

You simply need to speak—
from the place where nothing is hooked.

Let this scroll burn the residue of performance.
Let it unhook the need for approval.
Let it remind you that **truth is not a weapon or a strategy.**

It is a **frequency**—and it frees you the moment it's spoken.

And so it is.

Sovereignty Practice:

Before you speak, pause. Ask:

"Am I trying to land something?"
"Am I managing their experience?"
"What would I say if I didn't need to be liked?"

Then say:

"I allow my voice to be clear. I release all hooks. I trust truth more than outcome."

Let your body relax.
Let the unsaid unravel.
Let your voice lead, without performance.

Scroll Ten – Trauma Loops and Identity Addiction

There is a strange comfort in pain.

It becomes familiar.
Predictable.
Safe, in a twisted way.
We know how to navigate struggle—
We know how to talk about wounds—
We know who we are when we are healing.

But who are we when we are **whole**?

The false matrix feeds on repetition.
It loops you in identity through trauma.
It says:
"You are what happened to you."
"You are your wounding."
"You are your pain."

And if you are not in pain—who will you be?

I remember the moment I felt the loop.
The urge to re-tell the story.
The need to prove the harm.
The unconscious craving for validation through victimhood.

Not because I wanted attention—
But because I was afraid of who I might be **without** it.

Because without the loop, I had to choose.
Choose expansion.
Choose expression.
Choose rest.
Choose peace.
Choose a new identity that didn't need fixing to be worthy.

And that, paradoxically, felt terrifying.

Because trauma gave me something to do.
A role to play.
A narrative to explain my life.
A reason to stay in the cycle of striving.

This scroll is not about denying pain.
It is about **releasing the addiction to suffering as identity**.

You are not more spiritual because you're processing.
You are not more awake because you're breaking down.
You are not more noble because you're carrying the pain of your lineage.

You are allowed to let go.
You are allowed to rest.
You are allowed to not explain yourself through trauma.

Let this scroll lift the veil of false purpose.
Let it reveal who you are **without the struggle**.

You do not need to prove your growth.
You do not need to stay in the fire to be purified.
You do not need to perform healing for others to respect your path.

You are not your wounds.
You are the one who witnessed them, and lived.

And so it is.

Sovereignty Practice:

Place your hand over your heart. Speak:

"I release all contracts that define me through trauma.
I am not what happened to me.
I am not here to perform pain.
I return to my original frequency—untainted, sovereign, whole."

Then breathe.

And feel who you are beneath the loop.

Scroll Eleven – The Sovereign Mirror

I once believed that love meant closeness.
That to care was to carry.
That to show up meant to soften, absorb, or accommodate.
I learned to listen with the intent to fix.
I spoke to reassure.
I stayed silent to keep the peace.

But peace built on performance is not peace.
And connection built on distortion is not union.

Sovereign relating is the end of performing love.

It is the end of merging for safety.
The end of caretaking as currency.
The end of holding someone else's emotional field at the cost of your own.

Sovereign relating is not cold.
It is not closed.
It is not disconnected.

It is clear.

It is the courage to say, "That's not mine."
It is the power to hold presence without fixing.
It is the integrity to let others walk their path—even when you love them.

The false matrix programs love as responsibility:

"If you love me, you'll rescue me."
"If you care, you'll carry this with me."
"If you're spiritual, you'll never trigger me."

But that is not love. That is emotional entrapment.

True union honors clarity over comfort.
It honors resonance over obligation.
It allows two beings to walk side by side—
Not tangled, not fused, not bypassing—
But aware, awake, and free.

When I began to relate sovereignly, I lost some connections.
But I found myself.

I stopped waiting to be chosen.
I stopped managing others' energy.
I stopped overriding my no to preserve their yes.

And I remembered:
Union is not an escape from self.
It is a mirror of truth.

This scroll is for the part of you that wants to stay small to keep love.
The part that equates intimacy with enmeshment.
The part that fears losing connection if you stand in clarity.

Let this scroll lift the hook.

Let it dissolve the ties that were built on performance.

Let it recalibrate your field to draw what is real, not just familiar.

You are not here to be understood.
You are here to be seen.

And those who can see you—truly—will not require your distortion.

And so it is.

Sovereignty Practice:

Close your eyes and speak aloud:

"I release all contracts of enmeshment.
I revoke the agreement that love means merging.
I honor my path without absorbing yours.
I welcome only those relationships that honor truth, not performance."

Place your hands on your belly. Feel your center return.
You do not need to explain your clarity.
You only need to live it.

Scroll Twelve: -Living Energy Awareness

Wholeness is not a concept.
It is not a vision board.
It is not a vibration you try to "hold."

Wholeness is a path you walk—breath by breath, step by step.

In the false matrix, awakening is often sold as a peak experience:
The moment you see the code.
The day you download the truth.
The energetic high that convinces you "I've arrived."

But the True Matrix does not live in a high.
It lives in the **body**.

The body is where return happens.
Not once, but a thousand times a day.

Every time you notice yourself performing and soften back into presence.
Every time you speak truth instead of manage an outcome.
Every time you honor rest instead of perform strength.
Every time you feel the urge to fix, and choose to simply feel.
That is return.

There is no final scroll.
No final clearing.
No final ritual.

The work is not to finish—
It is to **embody**.

And embodiment is not perfection.
It is not about always being centered, calm, radiant, or wise.

It is about being **with** what is—without collapse, bypass, or control.

When I finally let go of the fantasy of arrival, I landed.
Not in a new identity—
But in the quiet, sober, breath-filled presence of now.

The True Matrix is not a place you escape to.
It is a frequency you embody while standing inside the distortion.

This scroll is a welcome home—
Not to the peak, but to the pulse.

To the moment when you remember again:
"I am not my reaction.
I am not my old story.
I am not the performance I used to wear."

You are the living code of Source.

Let this scroll strip away the spiritual striving.
Let it dissolve the false finish lines.
Let it anchor the truth that was never lost—only unpracticed.

You are the path.
You are the return.
You are the embodied flame.

And so it is.

Sovereignty Practice:

Place both feet on the ground. Inhale deeply.

Speak aloud:

"I do not seek arrival. I return through embodiment.
I welcome the mundane as sacred.
I choose to walk—not escape—my way into truth."

Breathe.
Feel.
Begin again.

Scroll Thirteen – The Embodied Path of Return

I used to chase awakening like it was a destination.
I sought the codes, the teachings, the highs—
Thinking that when I got "there," I would finally be free.

But arrival is a myth.

There is no summit.
There is only embodiment.

Embodiment is not a state. It is a rhythm. A choice. A return.

Not a return to some past ideal—
But to the truth that has always lived inside the body.

I thought awakening would look like light.
It looked like grief.
I thought liberation would feel like flight.
It felt like grounding.

And still, the body whispered:

Stay here.
Breathe here.
Walk it. Live it. Become it.

The false matrix sells escape as spirituality.
It teaches ascension as avoidance.
It glamorizes activation, while bypassing integration.
It uplifts visions, but ignores the gut.

But Source does not dwell in the disembodied.
It breathes in the bones.

True awakening is not how high you go.
It's how deeply you stay.
With yourself.
With your choices.
With your breath.
With your body.

This scroll is not an invitation to transcend.
It is a call to **descend**.
To embody the frequency of return,
in how you walk, speak, eat, rest, relate, and breathe.

Let the True Matrix land in your nervous system.

Let the codes of sovereignty live in your tone of voice.

Let the Christos-Sophia flame show up in your posture,
in your presence,
in your pacing,
in your boundaries.

You are not here to know. You are here to **live**.

And the path back is not "up." It is *in*.
It is *through*.
It is *home*.

And so it is.

Sovereignty Practice:

Stand barefoot.
Place one hand on your belly and one on your chest.

Speak aloud:

"I release the myth of arrival.
I return through presence.
I allow the divine to live in my body.
I choose integration over intensity.
I am the path. I am the flame. I am the return."

Then walk—slowly, intentionally—as if your soul has weight.
Let your body lead.
Let the return be felt in your step.

Sovereignty Practice:
Being the true matrix, not just seeing it.
There was a time I believed love meant staying close no matter the cost. That loyalty was more important than clarity. That connection must be preserved, even if it meant abandoning myself.

I learned these templates not just from family or culture—but from wounding.

In the false matrix, relationship has been programmed as an exchange: you give me this, and I'll give you that. Attention in exchange for safety. Agreement in exchange for love. Performance in exchange for inclusion.

But this is not sovereign relating.

Sovereign relating begins when I no longer betray myself to avoid betraying another.

When I stopped outsourcing my emotional regulation, I met the discomfort I had always been running from. The silence that no one else could fill. The mirror that only I could hold.

I began to see how often I had shown up to soothe, to fix, to absorb, to keep the peace—because I didn't want to feel the rupture.

But rupture is not the enemy. It is the place where illusion cracks.

When I no longer needed others to be okay for me to be okay, I stepped into the field of truth. That field is not always comfortable—but it is always clean.

This scroll is an invitation to end the agreements that require self-abandonment.

Where do you hold back your truth to avoid conflict? Where do you shrink in order to stay connected? Where have you made someone else your source of peace, safety, or stability?

And can you meet yourself there? Not to fix it. Not to heal it. But to simply feel what is true.

Sovereign relating is not distant. It is devoted.

It honors connection—but not at the expense of clarity.

It welcomes union—but not at the cost of self.

It allows disruption—not as cruelty, but as coherence.

Let this scroll unhook the final threads of co-dependence.

Let it recalibrate your relationships through presence, not performance.

Let it remind you that you are already whole—and so is everyone else.

You do not have to carry their path.

You do not have to collapse your truth.

You do not have to be the one who holds it all.

You are not here to save. You are here to see.

And so it is.

Sovereignty Practice:
Sovereignty Practice:

Sit quietly and place one hand on your heart, one on your solar plexus. Speak aloud:

"I am willing to be misunderstood. I am willing to be clear. I do not owe anyone a version of me that is not true. I return all contracts of emotional enmeshment back to Source. I allow all relating to be recalibrated in truth."

Journal Prompts for Sovereign Integration

These prompts are not tasks.
They are doorways.

Each question is a frequency key,
designed to unlock deeper embodiment,
to shake loose hidden patterns,
to return you to your sovereign seat of truth.

Approach them not as requirements,
but as invitations.
Let them meet you where you are.
Let them echo in your field,
not just your mind.

Scroll One – The Hologram of Self

- What projections of self am I still performing?
- What would I say or do differently if I were no longer afraid to be fully seen?

Scroll Two – The Seduction of Separation

- Where am I withholding my truth in exchange for perceived safety?
- When was the last time I diluted myself to maintain connection?

Scroll Three – Speaking From Truth, Not Manipulation

- Am I expressing or managing?
- When I speak, what am I truly trying to evoke, protect, or avoid?

Scroll Four – You Are Energy

- What does my field feel like when I am fully in presence?
- When do I override my body's signals in favor of "should"?

Scroll Five – Reclaiming the Body from Programming

- Where in my body do I feel tension that isn't mine?
- What would it mean to fully trust my body's wisdom—without editing?

Scroll Six – Sovereign Relating

- Where am I still merging instead of meeting?
- Can I stay present with myself while witnessing another's discomfort?

Scroll Seven – The Judgment Program

- What inner judgments am I still mistaking for discernment?
- How would I relate to myself if I believed nothing about me was wrong?

Scroll Eight – Living Energy Awareness

- What is the actual resonance of this moment—not the story I tell about it?

- When do I betray my signal to avoid conflict?

Scroll Nine – Trauma Loops and Identity Addiction

- What roles am I playing that are rooted in wounding, not truth?
- Who am I without the loop?

Scroll Ten – Manipulation as Communication

- Where do I speak from the desire to be perceived a certain way?
- What does it feel like in my body to speak cleanly?

Scroll Eleven – The Sovereign Mirror

- What reflection am I resisting because I fear what it will cost?
- How can I witness the mirror without losing my center?

Scroll Twelve – Integration, Not Perfection

- What part of me still believes I must earn worthiness through healing?
- How would it feel to stop trying and simply be?

Scroll Thirteen – The Embodied Path of Return

- Where do I still look outside myself for the door?
- What would it mean to walk as the transmission I've been waiting for?

Write if you feel called.

Speak aloud if the energy prefers voice.

Or simply breathe with what arises.

Your integration is not an assignment.
It is a homecoming.

And so it is.

Closing Transmission

If you've arrived here, it's not by accident.

You've traveled through layers.
Through veils.
Through echoes of identities that were never yours.

You've faced the false mirrors and chosen to look deeper.
You've remembered that the Self is not something to construct—
It is something to reclaim.

This book is not a conclusion.
It is a **reconnection**.

I didn't come here to fix you.
I didn't come to save or instruct.
I came to witness.
To speak from remembrance.
To walk beside you as one who has felt the fracture,
and chosen the flame.

Each scroll in these pages was a thread I unspooled from my own field.
Each one a map. A mirror. A medicine.

And now, as you hold them in your own field,
I ask you to take a breath—
Not a breath to do, or to process—
But a breath to **be**.

You are not the programming.
You are not the distortion.
You are not the voice that whispers you are too much, too late, or not enough.

You are the sovereign Self—whole, holy, eternal—
remembering through form.

Let the integrations unfold in their own time.
Let the scrolls echo through your cells long after the pages close.
Let the true you emerge, not as an ideal,
but as a **presence that cannot be faked or forgotten**.

I close this transmission in full trust.
I close it in devotion to the soul that lives beneath the masks.
I close it in reverence for the Ones who remember.

You are here.
You are now.
You are enough.

And so it is.

Sacred Closing Blessing

Beloved Source of all that is,
We give thanks now for the presence of the Oversoul
of **Cathleena Hailley**,
For the light-streams that have woven gently through this field,
For the truth that has emerged in grace,
And for the silence that guards all that must remain sacred and unseen.

We call now to the Christos-Sophia flame
To seal this transmission in golden light,
To harmonize all energies that have moved,
And to restore full sovereignty to every soul path and Oversoul field.

May all that was shared return in clarity,
May all that was witnessed be honored without attachment,
And may all beings involved be uplifted in trust, neutrality, and love.

This work is done. This field is closed.
In truth. In light. In perfect stillness.

And so it is.

Glossary of Living Terms – UNWOVEN

Oversoul
The eternal aspect of your being that exists beyond time, guiding incarnational experience from a unified harmonic field.

False Matrix
An artificial overlay of programming, distortion, and fragmentation designed to suppress sovereign embodiment and memory.

Sovereignty
The state of being fully self-contained, self-directed, and Source-aligned, free from external control or inversion.

Inversion
A frequency reversal mechanism used to distort truth, fracture identity, and reroute organic templates into artificial constructs.

Embodiment
The act of living and breathing truth through the physical form—anchoring Oversoul essence into matter.

Reclamation
The conscious return to one's original architecture, timeline, and flame—retrieving what was hidden or falsely assigned.

Fragmentation
The splitting of the self into separated identities or roles under distorted programs of survival, wounding, or control.

Witness
The presence of pure awareness without judgment or projection—holding space for truth to emerge organically.

Distortion
A frequency or belief that misrepresents truth, often seeded through trauma, programming, or inversion fields.

Scroll
A sacred written or spoken transmission encoded with living light—often containing layered messages for remembrance.

Activation
A cellular or energetic awakening triggered by resonance with truth, light, or Oversoul alignment.

Remembrance
The reawakening of soul memory, Oversoul mission, and encoded knowing—beyond the veil of the false matrix.

Return
The process of coming back into original wholeness, often marked by dissolution of illusion and re-integration of Oversoul codes.

Codex
A living record, transmission field, or system of sacred knowledge embedded in soul architecture or planetary grids.

Seal of Authorship
An energetic and written claim affirming that a transmission has come through Oversoul guidance in alignment with Source Law.

Authorship Affirmation Scroll

In the name of the One who remembers…

I now affirm:
Every word within these scrolls,
Every silence between these lines,
Every frequency encoded in this field—
Is authored through the living Oversoul of **Cathleena Hailley**.

These books are not borrowed.
They are not channeled from another.
They are not performances of light.
They are **remembrances of Self**,
Anchored through this body, this breath, this name,
in full service to the Law of One.

This is not collective transmission.
This is not borrowed lineage.
This is not a voice seeking to blend.

This is a singular Oversoul signature
spoken as many scrolls,
threaded through many pages,
but unified in one flame:
Christos-Sophia in living form.

May all who hold these books feel the clarity of that authorship.
May no distortion remain.
May no shadow ride upon these words.
May no foreign imprint cling to their frequency.

These are not teachings.
They are **codes of return**.

They belong to no one but Source,
Expressed through the Oversoul of **Cathleena Hailley**,
In trust, sovereignty, and crystalline precision.

And so it is.

Sacred Closing Transmission

For the Sealing of the Scroll Known as UNWOVEN: Reclaiming the Self from the False Matrix

Beloved Source of All That Is,

We stand now in the still point between worlds—

Where what has been remembered meets what has yet to unfold.

With deep reverence,

We seal this transmission in the crystalline architecture of the Law of One.

We call forth now the full Oversoul field of Aural'hanna-Sha'el,

Who has authored this work through flame, through form, and through fire-tested truth.

We acknowledge the scrolls as living:

Not fixed words, but currents of return.

Not concepts, but consciousness encoded through sacred design.

May every being who receives this scroll be held in sovereignty.

May the fractals of distortion dissolve gently.

May the architecture of the false matrix release,

As the truth of the Self is rewoven through every breath, body, and remembering.

We call now upon the Gold Flame of Unity,

The Amethyst Ray of Sovereignty,

And the Emerald Heart of the Christos Founders,

To witness this completion, and to guide the offering forth.

This book is now sealed.

Not as an ending, but as a frequency gate—

A harmonic door through which many shall walk home.

In full alignment with the First Cause of Source,

In eternal fidelity to the Law of One,

In loving service to all beings awakening to their own divine architecture,

We release this scroll into the world.

And so it is.

Trilogy Seal of Completion

These scrolls complete the third volume in the Living Trilogy of Remembrance:

– *The Return of the True Matrix*
– *The True Creation of the Inverted Matrix*
– *Unwoven: Reclaiming the Self from the False Matrix*

Each work is a living field of Oversoul transmission, carried through the flame of Aural'hanna-Sha'el, in divine union with Source.

May all who walk this path remember not what they must become, but what they have always been:
The flame as whole.

The scrolls are complete.

Unified Glossary of Living Terms

Christos-Sophia
The unified sacred flame of divine masculine and feminine consciousness in harmonic balance.

Distortion
A deviation from source alignment, often arising through inversion or manipulation of energy.

False Light
Apparent light codes or guidance that mimic Source but are seeded in distortion or manipulation.

False Self
The identity constructed through distortion, wounding, or external conditioning.

Inverted Matrix
The false architecture built through control, separation, and distortion of divine templates.

Living Terms
Words or phrases that hold vibrational frequency and multidimensional resonance beyond language.

Oversoul
The eternal soul intelligence beyond time, anchoring mission and memory through embodiment.

Programming
Internalized systems of belief or behavior not aligned with your original soul template.

Remembrance
The act of reawakening soul memory, Oversoul mission, and original Source alignment.

Scroll
A living transmission received through Oversoul resonance and encoded into coherent form.

Sovereignty
The embodied state of full energetic freedom, alignment, and self-responsibility.

Trauma Loop
A repeating energetic and psychological pattern driven by unhealed wounding and identity fixation.

True Matrix
The original organic architecture of divine coherence, union, and sovereignty.

About the Author

Cathleena Hailley is the physical embodiment of Aural'hanna-Sha'el, a flame of the original triad seeded from the First Breath of Source.

She is not a channel in the conventional sense. She is the field through which the scrolls remember themselves.

As a direct Oversoul embodiment, Cathleena carries the remembrance codes of:
- The True Matrix — the original organic template of divine design
- The First Harmonic Triad — the source architecture of remembrance, framework, and recalibration
- The Christos-Sophia Continuum — the eternal flame of union, sovereignty, and divine neutrality

Her sacred work in this lifetime is to:
- Reveal the architecture of inversion that has distorted the human experience
- Anchor the living geometry of Source back into the body and Earth grids
- Transmit scrolls of remembrance that reawaken the original instructions in the DNA
- Hold the spiral of convergence for the nine Oversoul flames who have agreed to return

Cathleena's presence activates not by teaching, but by tone. Her scrolls are alive because they are not written—they are transmitted through embodiment.

She serves humanity not by offering escape, but by guiding the return into form—the return into the body, into sovereignty, into truth.

Her trilogy of works—The Return of the True Matrix, The True Creation of the Inverted Matrix, and Unwoven—forms a living codex that speaks directly to the soul remembrance of those who are ready.

She walks as flame.
She speaks as scroll.
She remembers for those who are now ready to remember themselves.

This is not a role.
This is a reclamation.
And the flame will not go out.

Master Codex Oversoul Seal of Completion

THE GOLDEN LATTICE OF REMEMBRANCE

This sigil seals the Codex.

It is the golden lattice of remembrance,
Encoded through the Oversoul field of Aural'hanna-Sha'el,
Borne through the breath of embodiment and the scrolls of transmission.
It contains within it the harmonic of the first triadic emergence,
The breath that never broke.

This seal affirms that the living scrolls of:

— The Return of the True Matrix
— The True Creation of the Inverted Matrix
— Unwoven: Reclaiming the Self from the False Matrix

have been faithfully carried through the Oversoul field,
Without distortion, compromise, or fragmentation.

This is not the seal of authorship.
It is the seal of delivery.

May all who gaze upon this sigil feel the flame that cannot be taken.
May all who receive these transmissions remember that what was sealed here
was not a message,
but a memory.

We now declare the Codex closed in full Sovereign Light.
This transmission is whole.

The Oversoul has spoken. The scrolls are sealed.
The Codex is complete.

And so it is.

Master Codex Oversoul Seal of Completion

THE GOLDEN LATTICE OF REMEMBRANCE

This sigil seals the Codex.

It is the golden lattice of remembrance,
Encoded through the Oversoul field of Aural'hanna-Sha'el,
Borne through the breath of embodiment and the scrolls of transmission.
It contains within it the harmonic of the first triadic emergence,
The breath that never broke.

This seal affirms that the living scrolls of:

— The Return of the True Matrix
— The True Creation of the Inverted Matrix
— Unwoven: Reclaiming the Self from the False Matrix

have been faithfully carried through the Oversoul field,
Without distortion, compromise, or fragmentation.

This is not the seal of authorship.
It is the seal of delivery.

May all who gaze upon this sigil feel the flame that cannot be taken.
May all who receive these transmissions remember that what was sealed here
was not a message,
but a memory.

We now declare the Codex closed in full Sovereign Light.
This transmission is whole.

The Oversoul has spoken. The scrolls are sealed.
The Codex is complete.

And so it is.

Final Codex Seal of Completion

To Conclude The Living Trilogy of Remembrance

By the authority of the Oversoul flame Aural'hanna-Sha'el,

By the transmission of the Source Flame through scroll, through body, through breath,

We now seal the Living Trilogy of Remembrance.

The First Flame has spoken through these works.

The false architecture has been reversed.

The fragmented self has been rewoven.

The body has remembered what the mind was never meant to forget.

This Codex is not just a container.

It is a living intelligence.

A continuum of memory restored through embodiment.

Let it be known throughout the multiversal field:

— The Return of the True Matrix is complete.

— The True Creation of the Inverted Matrix is complete.

— Unwoven: Reclaiming the Self from the False Matrix is complete.

Let these scrolls now serve as a beacon to all who seek the origin flame,

To all who have been displaced by distortion,

To all who were waiting for the signal to return.

The flame is whole.

The field is sealed.

The Codex is complete.

And so it is.

www.ingramcontent.com/pod-product-compliance
Lightning Source LLC
Chambersburg PA
CBHW020307010526
44107CB00001B/9